Empowerment Through Knowledge Presents:

Why Real Couples Drink Straight Tequila

The Tao of Commitment
A Handbook for Couples in the New Millennium

Sarina Stone

TABLE OF CONTENTS

Dedication

This book is dedicated to Chi Kids Incorporated, a non-profit organization dedicated to teaching children and families about natural health through art, literature, and instruction.

Acknowledgement

Special thank you to Sheila, Fabienne, Amy, and Dorothy Gale for their wonderful literary contributions.

Love and Gratitude to Eric Thurnbeck for donating Chapter 2.

Thank you to Deb Schoenack for line edits and expert advice.

Much appreciation to Stan O'Daffer for tireless publishing efforts and a beautiful cover.

Introduction

Today I sit at my trusty Mac and offer to you an extension of the first book I wrote. By extension, I mean quite simply that all the rules from The Tao of Intimacy apply to The Tao of Commitment. Armed with knowledge, we enter a new dimension in the forthcoming text: committing to an extraordinary romantic relationship.

Sarina Stone
Author, Why Real Women Drink Straight Tequila – The Tao of Intimacy

Chapter 1

Taoist Quantum Manifestation
Connecting to the Source

In our first book we discovered that if we jumped into a theoretical boat named Taoist Quantum Manifestation and followed the stream of consciousness into the theoretical dating pool, we could find ourselves committed, theoretically, to someone healthy. That's a whole lot of theory, isn't it? Let's get practical.

Even if you're still working on your dating skills, this book will help you when you're ready to settle down.

So, for those of you who have a partner, let's talk about it. Let's pour ourselves a nice glass of tequila, open our mind, and absorb the Tao of Commitment.

Like all things Tao...

Cultivating, refining, and moving forward from dating mode to monogamy mode is a conscious effort, and like meditation, requires time to unfold. Each step in the cultivation process, for example, holds potential for another step on the road of personal enlightenment. The particles of reality generated from being together can be as awesome as the waves of possibility we danced with during courtship. Indeed, the sensations which occur when one feels love, honor, respect toward oneself, another, or the Universe is medicine to the body and brings about bliss, elation and lightness of being.

Right?

When you, dear reader, consider the vulnerability and deep connection one must abide in order to maintain love, how does it make you feel? Relaxed? At home?

Horrified?

If it's true that what we image we create, then it stands to reason that we must train our minds to embrace joy, love and unlimited potential as the norm. We must remember that we are on this planet, in this body, for such a short time; each moment of each experience is precious. In all of history, the enlightened sages have never found a replacement for the joy brought about by the Chi of Love. Not the stories or value assessments attached to the concept of love, but the actual Chi produced when a human being exercises their birthright to create this most amazing energy.

We become what we think about most of the time.

–William James

But what do we do to maintain this love?

Someone I know says "It's possible we're just elaborate chemistry sets with vivid imaginations." This statement used to rile the heck out of me.

As the years pass and my experience with Taoist meditation slowly unfolds, I see this statement as being based on fact. Mental transmutation was discovered, studied, and shared amongst scholars thousands of years ago. The Hermetic philosophy of ancient Egypt and Greece teaches us that anything and everything is transmutable. What's more, the vehicle that transforms this anything and everything is the mind. Indeed, the mind itself may be transmuted from state to state.

The old legends of turning base metal into gold are based on this ancient knowledge.

"Mind, (as well as metals and elements) may be transmuted, from state to state; degree to degree; condition to condition; pole to pole; vibration to vibration.

True Hermetic Transmutation is a Mental Art." – The Kybalion[1]

Psych 101 teaches that first we must find our own inner peace and joy, and then we can share it. The Tao agrees.

---

1   The Kybalion – page 43 (Three Initiates, Yogi Publication Society, 1912)

Laozi said,

If you let yourself be blown to and fro, you lose touch with your root. If you let restlessness move you, you lose touch with who you are.

- Tao Te Ching[2]

2   Tao Te Ching, Pocket version – page 26 (Stephen Mitchell, Harper Perennial, 1992)

But, what does it mean?

In this era of distraction and disconnection to the self, we not only lose touch with ourselves, but we have a tendency to become dependant on outside stimuli to feel whole.

"You complete me." Nice line in a sweet movie, but not particularly practical. If I need you to complete me, then I'm pretty screwed if you change your priorities, leave or pass away. I become incomplete if you don't comply.

A healthy relationship is the by-product of two separate, but whole people. If you can be alone without being lonely, you can be in a relationship without being a succubus. Boring, but true. I'm not being un-romantic. I'm actually giving you a powerful key, which unlocks a door to a place where loneliness cannot exist.

This book is about commitment. It is not about simply making a pledge to another person and then struggling not to break it. It is about being smart about what we commit to.

Reminder:

I remind you that these principals are not transient. You don't get to play by them for a while and then turn on a dime when something shiny catches your eye.

Remember Trixie? She was our adulteress. Trixie lied to everyone all the time. She married and cheated. She cheated and lied. No one really knows her because she is a complete fraud and she knows it. She is ill and will require much help if she is ever to be truly at peace in this lifetime.

Trixie has a sister, Dixie. Dixie doesn't cheat on her husband. Dixie seems to be a very sweet and servile woman. But, beneath the surface, Dixie is completely untrustworthy. Why? Because Dixie is also a fraud. Someone is always out to get Dixie and she can't figure out why. Maybe it's because in order to be right about how awful people are she has to manipulate the situation to turn people into monsters. So, Dixie lies about how she feels, then gets angry that she was "pressured" into situations, breaks 90% of her commitments, says what she thinks others want to hear (but doesn't mean it) and vilifies anyone who calls her out on her behavior. Yes, she's a lot like Trixie in that she is at heart a liar, but her presentation is different. Where Trixie just loses the respect and love of her lovers, Dixie has lots of friends, but keeps them at arm's length. If they don't leave her because her word means nothing, they leave her because eventually, she behaves like a caged animal and attacks anyone who gets too close to her truth. A snake by any other name would smell as slimy. The only people who stay in Dixie's life for an extended period are those who play the same game. Water seeks its own level. So Dixie, like her sister, is committed to remaining paranoid and shameful, no doubt due to some emotional trauma as a youth.

One Dixie I know has a pattern of being gooey sweet to people and then vilifying them and attacking them after she gets to know them. She has no friends, yet on the surface, she seems like such a sweet person. She doesn't see that the common denominator in all of her negative dramas (and there is always something creepy in Dixie's life) is she! Dixie is forever losing relationships, staying safely isolated, and making her ill behavior someone else's fault.

Now, follow me here. I am not on a wild tangent. Based on results, Dixie is committed to a) being betrayed and b) being abandoned. If Dixie (and Trixie) would commit to oh, let's say, telling the truth once in a while, there would be fewer shenanigans but there would also be a deeper level of intimacy between them and all things. The loneliness would fade as honest and true connections were created.

How about committing to a belief system based on integrity and human kindness? Wow. Wouldn't that change the landscape for our sisters?

Commitment is not just a romantic issue. It is a human issue and thus must be entered into with gentleness and forethought.

And by the way, changing your mind after you have committed is valid and normal. We are adults. We are human beings. If we make a mistake and commit to something we hate once we're really in there, there are ethical ways to move on, and these will be discussed here. Commitments frequently present obstacles and as adults, we are expected to weather them with integrity.

So, if you're going to push forward with this text, know that you are allowed to make mistakes, change your mind, and even win once in a while. There is a backlash for every action you take, so commit to being a decent human being who is worthy of all the love this life has to offer.

Back to the point

Okay, where were we? Ah yes, being smart about what we commit to. It would stand to reason that if a person wants to be in love, and be happy inside of that, that all they would need to do is visualize this end. It makes sense to simply hold the thought of a successful future. But alas, as humans, we tend to miss the path of least resistance and complicate everything.

We image a beautiful face. We image a nice body. Some image a hardy bank account. The list goes on and on. So, we get fragments of what we really want. Or do we? Do we feign ignorance in order to stay disappointed and alone?

The answer is that some of us are very busy distracting themselves with pointless endeavors in an effort not to get too close to another person. We spoke on that extensively in "The Tao of Intimacy". If you haven't read it, you should. That being said, some of us honestly just need a little advice on how to use their ability to manifest. Volumes on this subject have been written and more volumes are coming.

Here, we only care about manifesting one thing; a fulfilling romantic relationship. And folks, there's only one way to stay committed to a relationship with anyone and like it. You must have a healthy romantic relationship with yourself and something bigger than you first. Oh! Sounds like religion! No! Calm down. It's not that dogmatic and it certainly isn't that complicated.

We've all heard that in order to love someone else, you have to love yourself first. This is most certainly true. But where does this love come from? Thin air? A statue? Mom? Dad?

A Taoist would stay out of debate on whether or not there is a higher power or creator. A perception of God is personal, so there really is no argument being that a point of view is subjective. We accept that our lives are an expression of interaction between the Universe and ourselves. Some of us like to call this Universe "The Source". My teacher, Master Mantak Chia, always tells his students to connect to The Source for answers to their problems. It must be working because he is the most published living teacher on Taoist meditation in the world.

The Source

This Source never lies, never leaves, and is in action in our lives 24/7. We may feel safe and secure in our relationship with this Source as it doesn't change its mind about being there for us. It simply reflects our deepest beliefs and is ever steadfast in its miraculous ability to manifest what's on our mind into real form. Through building faith in something bigger than ourselves we may connect to the energy of the mother, father, brother and sister. We may choose to experience this Source as a love that knows no time or restriction. We may choose to learn about unconditional kindness and put it into action in our lives because this Source rewards us in kind. We may see love reflected in everything and everyone.

We all have access to this Source of love, and through it, we may experience peace and trust. A person who is adored by the Source could never feel incomplete, even if another human being leaves them.

This is a lofty wish, never to feel abandoned, but it is a wise one. Without the need for others to complete you, you are free to enjoy what they bring to your life and you won't feel slighted when their behavior is less than accommodating. In other words, we may accept others just the way they are. This is a healthy first step in manifesting a person whose love is a mirror for this type of existence.

Hocus pocus demystified - The Projection Infection

So, you finally met someone you could love and lo and behold, they love you back. It's the greatest gift you ever got. Every love song on the radio is about you. Birds chirp gleefully as you and your beloved walk hand in hand down the street. It's like frickin' Disney over there.

Hey, if you've ever been in love, you know it's really like that. All jokes aside, there are few experiences more profound than being in love with someone who loves you back. The ability to love and be loved is one of the greatest gifts we may experience as human beings. Songs and poetry have been written for thousands of years because of this great gift. They say wars have been fought over love, but I can't imagine pure love could generate such atrocity.

So, how is it that responsible, self aware adults who loved each other enough in the beginning of their relationship to make a commitment to monogamy could repel each other or view each other so differently after a period of time?

There are many answers to this question. We will examine one of the biggest demons here.

As a personal coach I sit for hours a day and listen to people speak about what's wrong in their life. I am, in essence, a professional listener. By far the most common issue I find in relationships is "Projection". In this context, projection means that we have experiences that teach us what things mean, and this meaning tends to carry through to all other experiences until a new meaning comes along to replace it. But, let the thinker beware because "meaning" implies judgment, and judgment can be dangerous. Men and women frequently are not able to see each other clearly. They see an eye or hair color, a facial or body feature, or mannerism that may remind them of someone they once knew. Since the brain does not know the difference between what it is experiencing and what it remembers, we see projections so heavily that they become a mask covering the real face. We see, in essence, what we believe to be true, regardless of the reality contained in the heart and soul of the being.

A projection can be sweet or sour, and may cause great pleasure or pain. But, remember dear reader, a projection is still a projection –

not reality. For the projectionist, this illusion or mask prevents us from experiencing true intimacy.

For example, I once knew a woman who refused to put her children in a bathtub. They were allowed to shower or sponge bathe, but never allowed to soak in a tub. In an odd turn of events, this woman learned that when she was just a babe, her mother placed her in a tub so hot that she thought she was being boiled alive. Her mother misinterpreted the baby's screams and had no idea her child was in pain. From that point forward, this woman's judgment of bathtubs was that they were dangerous. No one could talk her out of it until she re-experienced the trauma in therapy and could process the experience as an adult. Today, she understands that the fear of bathing is an illusion or projection, and may use any number of techniques to calm her mind to reality; it's just a bath.

How do I know if I am projecting judgment onto another person?

Know yourself. Know your patterns and beliefs. Is this situation familiar? Is this what happens every time?

Remember, we become what we think about the most. This statement has layers of understanding. I find it fascinating that when a person has a specific mind-set, or belief, they will go to great lengths to make themselves right about what "always happens". If that doesn't work, they just see their story forming around them, even when it's not. We call these people crazy, unless they are rich. Then they are eccentric.

OK, here's another one of those pivotal, get your highlighting pen out statements. Ready?

The common denominator in all of your relationships is…you.

So, if people always disappoint, leave, or betray you, guess what? You are a crap magnet. You are a crap magnet because you believe in a lie that is hurting you. In order to manifest this pain, you must take a little crap from someone, don't you? Here's the big question. Which people were sincerely kind and loving and which ones were actually slingin' poo? You have to take responsibility for projecting crap on people who tried to love you as much as taking responsibility for manifesting crappy dates.

You used to be committed to repeating negative stories, but now, well, that's all changed. Right?

The good news and the other news are the same. If you can attract crap, you can attract blessings, joy and success. You can attract love once you stop focusing on loss. And that, my friend, is worth getting up, rolling up your sleeves and working toward.

Chapter 2

From author and personal coach, Eric
Thurnbeck…

_____

Greetings and salutations, readers. You may remember me from my contribution to Why Real Women Drink Straight Tequila : The Tao of Intimacy, in which I talked about my dating experiences with other men. My dear friend Sarina asked if I would be able to offer my thoughts on commitment for this book, and I was only too happy to oblige.

I've developed some theories about commitment over the years, which I am about to share with you. In addition to having a few of my own serious commitments under my belt, I've also counseled many other couples about their relationships, helping them to tune into one another's mindsets and arrive at greater truths.

Please read with an open mind, and feel free to take it with a grain of salt. I'm still figuring this out, just like everyone else.

What I have learned about commitment

We are all committed, in one way or another. Of course, the details of our commitments will vary, depending on who or what we commit ourselves to. Quite often, we forge commitments without really knowing it – simple habits can become commitments over time, and we only pay attention to them when the time comes for them to change.

When people talk about commitments, most of us connote the word with relationships, though this isn't always the case. We commit to our friends, our families, our careers, our ideals, and our educations just as deeply as we do to our lovers. Ideally, our relationship commitments will be direct manifestations of our other commitments, but sometimes we put the cart before the horse.

One of the most difficult things I've learned is this: without a clear understanding of what I am committed to myself, I won't be very successful in committing to other people. As selfish as it sounds, our own goals will usually supersede our involvement with the goals of others, and if we're not committed to the right things, we end up with the wrong people.

The first challenge of unraveling the meaning of our commitments is having the knowledge of where they come from. It might seem silly, but asking ourselves questions about our commitments' origins is vital to understanding how they interrelate to the various facets of our lives, and more importantly, why they're important to us in the first place. This requires us to know what we are truly committed to as individuals.

Sit back and ask yourself: What am I committed to? What do I consider important? How do these commitments shape my day-to-day life?

The answers to these questions will say a lot about you and your attitude about relationships. The answers are neither good nor bad on their own, but if you're uncomfortable examining them, that means you probably need to take a deeper look. Your commitments are the underpinning of everything you do, including and especially how you relate to others.

If you're not sure what you're committed to, take a look at your life – your present circumstances are a direct manifestation of your choices and commitments. For some of us, this may be a tough pill to swallow, but there it is.

There is a temptation to pass the origins of our commitments onto people and factors outside ourselves – some of us are prone to say we're committed to certain ideas because of how we were raised, or we find ourselves in relationships of convenience and remain committed because it's comfortable. This type of passive attitude is ultimately self-defeating, because we can't ever truly commit to something or someone we didn't choose for ourselves.

The solution, of course, is to take an active, rather than passive role. The teachings of the Tao and of Quantum Manifestation indicate that the images we construct in our minds will be manifested in reality over time. If you're not happy with what you see, you can take it upon yourself to see something different, and changes will begin to take place.

The truth is that commitment is one of the greatest challenges we face. If we can rise to the occasion that is presented, we stand to gain a great deal, but it requires a deep and consistent self-honesty that can seem intimidating. Only you can decide whether or not the truth is worth facing, but if you do, be prepared for a lot of hard work that will ultimately yield immense and lasting reward.

So how does all of this work?

Of course, the particulars of commitments will vary from person to person, and couple to couple. I've borne witness of many commitment strategies and ideas – some successful, others, not so much.

Some of the most challenging and valuable lessons about commitment that I have learned have been demonstrated by a client and good friend of mine, a man slightly younger than I am named Nathan.

Nathan and I began talking about his relationships a few years ago, when he was looking to change the direction of his love life. He'd had a few unsuccessful forays into romantic partnership, much like I had. He wanted to commit to something deeper and more meaningful, but he wasn't sure how to approach it.

We started by examining what he was looking for, and upon reflection, he realized that he'd previously chosen men who were safe for one reason or another, who were unlikely to abandon or betray him. While of course this is important to everyone, Nathan focused almost exclusively on the concept of security, and remained committed specifically to have a man – any man – in his life.

Nathan's commitment to the idea of security led him to overlook a host of other potential issues with the men he chose. One boyfriend was extremely passionate and spontaneous, but so focused on him that their relationship bordered on psychological dependence, creating a bottomless need that Nathan had no hope of filling. Another was certainly handsome and charming, but he was also jobless and irresponsible, more than content to remain with Nathan while Nathan paid his rent. A third was successful and well put together, but he was demanding, controlling, and attacked Nathan's self-esteem.

Each of these relationships eventually ended with Nathan walking away, frustrated and disillusioned by his experiences. When we talked, I identified a consistent feeling of action without result; he was spinning his wheels in an emotional quagmire, without ever moving forward.

Each time we met, he would ask me, "What am I doing wrong?"

We consulted the I Ching, and the answer was Hexagram 32, Heng, or Duration.

This passage of the I Ching is often described as a mountain, representing the need to weather difficulty with steadfastness and an adherence to the current course. This seemed to be a double-edge sword in Nathan's case, he was doing his best to commit, to find a relationship and stick with it, giving it time to grow and mature, but on the other hand, his commitment to commitment had blinded him to the ways in which he had betrayed himself. In allowing his need for a romantic partnership to override his need to value and protect himself he sabotaged his work toward wholeness.

Nathan is alone for now, but he has realized that he needs to know what he is truly committed to in order to manifest the relationship that will best suit his needs. His internal choices have been mirrored by his circumstances all along, and now his challenge is to make the correct choices and to stick with them – just as the I Ching advised.

What we should examine:

Even though Nathan's story hasn't ended with a Happily Ever After,
it shouldn't be regarded as a defeat either. He has actually expressed
gratitude that he has been given the opportunity to examine his life in an
authentic way, and he refuses to shut his mind down and settle into something simply for the sake of not being alone. He has committed himself to
the pursuit of truth and the deepest wholeness possible, which can sometimes be uncomfortable, but is always ultimately rewarding.

What we can all do is examine our own commitments from the ground up,
and they will give us an idea of why our relationships work the way they
do. We are the creators of our own realities, and we choose the commitments that govern our lives.

Look at what's around you. This is the life you have envisioned for
yourself, for better or worse, and only you can change it. What we image,
we create, and the key to lasting wholeness is to imagine a life in which
wholeness can be obtained.

When you envision the future in which you feel the happiest, don't leave
anything out. Commit to all of it. Each piece can be achieved on its own
and over time, they can be woven together into the reality of your choosing. We will all be perpetual works in progress, but with proper adherence
to the process, we can find the rewards we seek and others who seek what
we do.

And when they arrive, we can commit to share what we've learned.

Chapter 3

Avoidance Behavior 101

It's so easy to spot someone who is avoiding intimacy. Or is it?
Most of us think of avoidance as an outright refusal to participate in an activity or endeavor. But if we really take a look at avoidance, we find it can be cloaked in so many ways.

We make ourselves busy. We surround ourselves with others and delve into their lives. We work. We over-commit. We get too tired. We get too wired. We travel. We get sick. These are clever techniques to avoid the things that matter at home.

This chapter is about the importance of being present in your relationship, even when it's uncomfortable - especially when it's uncomfortable.

I have interviewed countless couples and asked most of them what makes their relationships work. The healthy, happy couples all agree that they have a special communication between them and that this openness is part of what makes their relationship work. Without fail, each couple also agrees that they feel a sense of giving and support from their partners, which actually makes the craziness of life easier to tackle. They are a team, and this camaraderie is part of the glue that binds them.
But, what happens when one or both partners emotionally shut down and are unavailable for a spell?

Some people shut down when they feel, on a deep level, that they cannot handle their own truths. For example, when people are dealing with failure (especially financial or professional failure) and this failure affects their home lives, they may feel pressured and embarrassed that they are inconveniencing their partners. They may keep the details of the loss a secret from their partners for a period of time in the hope things will work themselves out. But, sometimes things don't work themselves out. Sometimes we fail to accomplish our goals the first time we give it a shot. Sometimes a failure is just a lesson and a stepping-stone to success. But, when people create secrets, they also create walls between themselves and their partners.

In order to relax, these people now need to separate themselves from their partners. It takes energy to maintain space between them and that which confronts them, so being around their partner is now work. Unable let their guard down, they can't fully relax, trust and just be. Thus, avoidance begins.

That's just one example. Most of us have areas of emotional discomfort. There are a million reasons to avoid these areas. But there is one strong reason to plow through theses fears and share them with the partner who loves you and wants to be close to you, even when you're not doing well.

Exploring the world is a wonderful thing, but there's no place like home, and if we do not do the work to maintain healthy foundations with our partners, some day we may come home and find our cozy nests empty; even if our partners are physically there.

Avoiding that which makes us uncomfortable is human, and as we mature, we tend to get more creative in how we avoid confrontation. So, lovers beware. Be careful not to let too much time go by without stopping to check in with your partner. Set private time aside each week for each other. Share your thoughts and ask your partner to do the same. Listen. Shut off the phone for a few hours. Bond.

Making time for yourself and your partner is just as important as keeping your professional associations and commitments, so be mindful when creating your mental list of priorities. Remember, at the end of the day you can't hug your job.

Chapter 4

Gratitude

To educate oneself for the feeling of gratitude means to take nothing for granted; to always seek out and value the kind that will stand behind the action.

Nothing that is done for you is a matter of course.
Everything originates in a will for the good, which is directed at you.

Train yourself never to put off the word or action for the expression of gratitude.

-Albert Schweitzer[1]

1   - http://www.wisdomquotes.com/002941.html

Gratitude is probably the most important ingredient in maintaining a healthy committed relationship. If we could stop and make a check-list of all the things we have for which to be grateful in the middle of a fight, many fights would end before they became destructive. There was a reason you were attracted to this person in the first place. You used to be grateful for the little things. "He took the garbage out." Joy! "She made the bed." That is so hot!

I have a friend, a bonafide guru actually, who never ceases to amaze me with his luminous gratitude and humility. I've seen him smile through what appears to be loss and turmoil. I've seen him gently remove himself when a situation becomes toxic, and allow himself the luxury of a broken heart until he can see the light again. My friend has trained himself to find the lesson in times of adversity. He can be grateful for the opportunities that arise when doors close, because he knows a window to somewhere else is opening simultaneously.

The best part of spending time with this man is that when there is no conflict, he holds the same level of gratitude. He can marvel at a plant or butterfly with the same grace he marvels at his own humanity.

What I learned about gratitude from spending time with this man is to start with the self. (Hmmm, we've heard that before, haven't we?) Gratitude is an internal state; it can only be nurtured and grown through careful self-cultivation.

We must remember that each thought we hold is an opportunity to live in joy and happiness or remain bound to old, negative patterns. As human beings, we are blessed to be at choice 24/7. In the Tao, we believe that our external lives are mere reflections of our internal situations, so wise people take their thoughts into consideration before harboring them too long.

Here is a check list to becoming a great partner:

Be grateful for the little things.

Make a conscious effort to do something kind every day, and don't tell anyone you did it. Communication happens in the response you get.

Become someone others could appreciate.

Try saying thank you once in a while.

Set a good example.

Water seeks its own level, so think before you judge.

Chapter 5

Expectations, Money and Responsibility

"Failure is an opportunity.
If you blame someone else, there is no end to the blame.
Therefore the Master fulfills her own obligations
and corrects her own mistakes.
she does what she needs to do
and demands nothing of others."
-Laozi Tao Te Ching[1]

1   Tao Te Ching by Stephen Mitchell, Published by Harper and Row, 1988. Page 79

I cannot count how many times I have sat across from a man or woman while they droned on about how utterly lacking their boyfriend's / girlfriend's / spouse's financial intelligence is. Words like irresponsible, reckless, thoughtless, and childish fill my office like a heavy cloud some days. It never ceases to amaze me how people take each other's poor behavior personally either.

The other day-to-day issue I hear about is general thoughtlessness or irresponsible behavior, i.e. keeping commitments, self-care, and general planning skills.

So, I'm going to share another key to commitment in this piece. Listen very carefully and note each of the following words...

People don't joyfully change because someone tells them they have to. They change because they are inspired to do so.

Positive change comes from an internal realization that we want more for ourselves or those we love.

Do you know the story of the sun and the wind? In case you don't, the sun and the wind have a competition to see who is stronger. They choose a man walking down a long road and decide to see who can remove the man's coat first. The wind won the coin toss and starts aggressively blowing as hard as it can. But, the harder the wind blows, the more the man clutches his coat to his chest. Eventually, the wind tires and tells the sun it has tried everything. Then, the sun takes its turn. It gently shines golden rays of warmth onto the now flustered man. Shortly, the man relaxes. Within minutes he removes his coat of his own volition, so he may enjoy basking in the sun as he walks.

I could beat this horse to death and mention that you catch more flies with honey, too, but that would be redundant.

What I will do is mention something an old friend taught me. In our past, he had to remind me a few times that growing the negative in him by boldly pointing out his faults and failures did not make him feel comfortable with sharing the deeper parts of himself with me. He felt attacked at times. And, since he is a man, Yin wrapped in Yang, he doesn't forget what that feels like.

Because I am 100% committed to being his trusted friend, I listened. I learned very quickly that in order to get what I want, his trust, I have to be a real friend and allow him to grow at his own pace. Furthermore, I need to help him grow the good by acknowledging what an amazing man he is, and showing support when he does make a change for the better. I need to celebrate his strengths and support him through the transformation of his self-sabotaging behaviors. And in return, I get to be a friend and confidant of a really wonderful and intelligent man. I win.

However, prior to being so smart and sensitive, I was just a young, stubborn woman. I was so stubborn that one year I calculated that I paid over 1/3 of my income to the California Department of Motor Vehicles and the Los Angeles Police Department. Why? I refused to get automobile insurance. I also refused to stop speeding and driving recklessly. I wasn't stupid, just irresponsible. When I look back, I drove the way I felt; pissed off.

The state of California was more than happy to let me be irresponsible and had no problem taking my money for the privilege. No one from the State gave me a huge lecture on the virtues of being a respectable citizen, they simply treated me like the immature person that I was. So, when I got a little older and purchased my first auto insurance policy, I was tickled when I got pulled over and could give the nice officer my proof of insurance. Unfortunately it took another 10 years, thousands of dollars, and two license revocations for me to stop speeding. I guess I'm a slow learner. But, ultimately, I understood the freedom that comes from having nothing to hide. I learned this through trial and error and drew my own conclusions. It just had to be that way. Is there anyone out there feeling my vibe?

So, if your sweetheart loves you; treats you with kindness, listens to your stories, and holds you when you need to be held, return the love and stop whining. If they can't balance a check book, make a dinner reservation or drive under the speed limit, maybe you can. That's what a partnership is. Life is better because you are a team. One cooks, the other does dishes. If this is your point of view, you will find yourself looking for the positive gifts your partner brings to the table and what you yourself can contribute in return. This attitude of gratitude helps us to build loving Chi instead of losing it through focusing on negativity. As always, the choice is yours.

What inspires such change?

Many of us are reckless when we are single and uncommitted. Our college days are a testament to that. If the only person we hurt is ourselves, who cares? It isn't until we commit to something or someone to which we want to bring something positive that we feel motivated to change.

For example, sometimes it isn't until a person falls in love with a person or a career that they experience the joy that comes from taking care of someone else. For me, it was the Tao and my Chi Kung practice. Chi Kung has led me back to humanity and revealed a great passion to make a difference with children, people and our planet. I can't do that if I bring negativity and drama to an already precarious world.

On Gender

Even though all men are different, the nature of man is to provide and protect. It's a cave man thing that has not been bred out. Some of the most shut down, devious men I've met have become the most committed, loving, responsible providers when they are inspired to do so. No one makes these men become trustworthy; they simply change their actions to facilitate the new life they now desire. They are committed to intimately sharing their life and don't want to ruin the relationship by bringing negative drama or poor credit to the table. Right, guys? I'm going to bat for you here. Make me proud...

In the same way, it is woman's nature to nurture and be taken care of. Oh! Come now, ladies. Calm down. I'm not saying we were bred to serve, but I am saying that some of the most powerful women in history have been kind, warm and generous toward their community, family, and those they love and respect. And remember, we make the babies, girls. It's normal to look at a partner and ask yourself if they may take care of you while you do this most incredible thing. Like water, loving, healthy women gently provide undying stability and support in any situation. They forgive. They embody compassion. They allow themselves to be taken care of and, in exchange, offer the same care and support to those around them. This is particularly difficult during PMS as our desire is to hunt things down and kill them, but, we try.

And in this space, we cultivate unconditional love. So even though our man or community is far from perfect, we love and support openly and with passion. This is an example of the balancing effects of Yin and Yang.

I saw something really wonderful the other day. I have a few friends in the entertainment industry. After a particularly long day performing, two fellas in a three man show decided to finish the day with beer; lots of it. Now, I was at the house we all shared for a couple of days when the boys came in. One of them was grey and could barely speak. His wife, bless her heart, gently took her near puking husband by the arm and put him to bed. The other gentleman did not need help, he headed straight for his room, and his wife simply checked on him, kissed his forehead, and let him sleep. I watched as the two women met in the kitchen to prepare dinner shortly after they had attended their husbands. I wondered if they were angry or disappointed. To my delight, these women were warm, humorous and sweetly attentive. Their gut instinct said, "Big daddy needs a little loving care tonight." And lovingly care for their men, they did. These men had just spent 2 days working their butts off for their families, and now it was their turn to be taken care of.

Can you see the healthy circle here? Can you see that with such love and respect, a partner may be inspired to be the best man he can be to protect his family from harm? It doesn't matter that underneath the professional exterior these men present to the public, they were adolescent in their after hours behavior. Their wives are very clear on where their husbands' strengths and weaknesses are, and signed on for the long haul anyway; because they love their husbands and accept them just the way they are.

Again, it would stand to reason that a man who values a healthy partnership would not want to threaten this beloved support. Thus, responsible actions which lead to a safe, and secure life just make sense. So, if the relationship is genuine, the same man who behaved recklessly and irresponsibly in his personal life will change his behavior simply because he wants to be respected, trusted and adored. He wants to be a better man.

Another thing to note for some men is that it is as energetically satiating to care for their woman and child as it is for a woman to be allowed to support those she loves. It's actually more fulfilling than the chase, capture, and sexual conquest they were dedicated to as a single man. Not all men react this way to being truly loved, but enough do that I am firmly convinced that even though some say marriage is becoming outdated, we will continue to honor this institution for a very long time.

If a couple cultivates the ability to open and receive the unique energy that is the by-product of trust and balance, they may taste a fine and intoxicating elixir called intimacy. They will want to drink this elixir whenever possible as it will give them strength on many levels.

So, remember that change happens internally and naturally, if it happens at all. All the harping and disapproval in the world will not hasten the harvest; so if you are a whiner and complainer, stop wasting your energy and start supporting your partner.

On the physical plane, just like I did, an intelligent person eventually gets sick of the bad credit, loss of money, anxiety and extra work involved with being a screw up. It hurts to feel our partner or associates separate themselves. It hurts to know others shut down parts of their connection because they want nothing to do with the mess. No one really needs to sit us down and tell us what a waste of energy being irresponsible is, we know. And, we change in our own time; or not.

How do we know if someone is capable of becoming financially or personally responsible?

"Be like water making its way through cracks. Do not be assertive, but adjust to the object, and you shall find a way round or through it. If nothing within you stays rigid, outward things will disclose themselves.

Be shapeless. Be formless like water.

When you pour water in a glass, it becomes the glass.

When you pour water into a cup, it becomes the cup.

When you pour water into a teapot, it becomes the teapot.

Water can flow, or water can crash.

Be water my friend."

-Bruce Lee[2]

Water seeks its own level, folks. If you open to your partner, and your partner opens to you, you will know the answer to this question. And soon enough, based on results, we see what is harbored in the heart of each man or woman. Whether or not you choose to stay in the relationship once you know the score is up to you.

[2]   Quote from http://www.fightingmaster.com

Regardless of gender, once committed to a partnership, if a person does not act conscientiously, then they are either uncaring for themselves, uncaring for those in their life, or an uneducated person who should seek council so they may change their results[3]*.

Couples who go into debt together tend to have the same issues. They also tend to blame each other for how they got there. Bottom line, when one person in the group does not play the victim and allow for their partners poor choices to diminish their quality of life, the partnership differs from those where both partners participate in the dysfunction. If just one of you is responsible or educated, there's hope for a positive transformation or growth as the result of the union. And yes, once in a while one partner messes up and both people suffer loss, but in general, if open communication and trust exist, there should not be any surprises, just choices.

As with all things Tao, start by knowing yourself. Then, know your partner. Watch the results of their actions before you commit 100% and combine your assets, lives and reputations. Does it come natural to you both to trust each other and share responsibility based on each others strengths and weaknesses? Are you setting each other up to be right about how inept the other person is? Are you both willing to bring out all of your paperwork, spread it on the table and show each other who you are on paper? Are you afraid of what your beloved would do if they knew the state of your affairs? Are you keeping secrets because you are embarrassed about your past or present situation in any arena (it takes a lot of energy to withhold, do you really have that much to spare)?

Again, this book is about commitment. What are you committed to and what are you willing to give up in order to get there?

The choice is yours.

---

3   * Mordant and I studied finances to improve our financial intelligence. We knew we wanted to bring this stability not only into our own lives, but in to our intimate relationships. We needed an education, and thus studied Napoleon Hill, Robert Kyosaki, T. Harv Ecker, and finally, Wallace Wattles.
If you really want to be a good partner, you owe it to yourself to make the commitment to financial freedom. You'll thank yourself later. This isn't a book about money, so, nuff' said.

What to do while the irresponsible party is learning through loss

It's so easy to focus on someone else's poor behavior, especially when their behavior inconveniences us.

So, here are a few thoughts on keeping it together during times when one or both of you are being stubborn and holding on to dysfunctional behavior which leads to loss or damage.

Keep it honest. Give your partner space to grow. If they fall down, let them pick themselves up, dust off, and try again. I know it's hard to watch someone you love screw up, but that's what is required some days. Be a good listener. Tell the truth and accept nothing less than honesty from your partner. Never belittle your partner for making choices that lead to loss (actually, I frequently find the look on my face to be reprimand enough). If possible, simply and openly separate yourself from the financial, legal or other trouble and allow your partner to suffer the repercussions of their own actions. Don't try to fix or save an adult.

If it's not possible to separate, you must examine how you let this happen to you and focus on yourself. You are the captain of your own ship, remember? There is no need for both of you to go down with that ship. As mentioned earlier it is possible that the feelings of separation will inspire the person behaving recklessly to take a look at their actions and repercussions. Then again, maybe not.

I wish I could say more. I wish I could tell you that your disappointment, pain or loss was enough to inspire your partner to stop the dysfunction immediately, but I can't. I can only tell you that during times when we doubt ourselves and the choices we made, we are in a most wonderful position; we get to grow. We get to be sad. We get to be vulnerable. We get to unlock a piece of ourselves previously hidden away and look that person in the eye.

If you ran into a Sufi and told them your woes, the Sufi would say, "You're in pain? You're having trouble? How wonderful!" And after you looked at her like she had three heads, she would say "Don't you see? Once you get through this barrier, you get to grow! You will resolve this issue and never be its victim again."

What I'm saying is that when you are in the presence of your partner during times of utter dysfunction, don't forget to look in the mirror daily. Who are you in the presence of weakness? Are you the Victim? Are you the Persecutor? Are you the Whiner and Complainer? Or are you an open person who holds the space for prosperity, love and success when your partner can't. Regardless, if there is a true desire for partnership, the rest will take care of itself.

The choice is yours.

Healthy Affirmations for Sharing Responsibility

- I support my partner's growth, and celebrate their victories.
- I have faith and image in the best possible outcomes for us both.
- I set a good example by being responsible and open to greater financial freedom every day.

Chapter 6

Fabienne's Story

My dear friend, Fabienne, is French so the English may not be perfect, but the story of how she found and kept love in her life is as perfect as I've ever seen.
Sarina

A chapter for my friend Sarina's book
 or how I became what I am…

"You think of it, you feel it, you do it!…"

An Australian Shaman

1st part: I know it's not my body.

Dear Reader, I had the honour of being asked to share this story with you. I hope you can recognize a part of yourself. It's nothing serious, just a little trick on the precious path of inner and outer transformation....

My name is Fabienne. Today, I am a Universal Healing Tao Senior Instructor, one of Master's Chia's vital force teachers. Sometimes on the path we can feel lonely. And it can be nice to have a good friend who shares a story to help you feel that magic can also be real...

The beginning of my spiritual awakening happened when I discovered that I was in a body that was not mine. It was a strange feeling. I looked at myself and I was sure it wasn't me. I didn't know who it was exactly. I looked at myself, I looked and looked, and I saw a body I didn't like. I couldn't like it because it wasn't mine. My body has always played an important role in my life. My transformation story begins with the fact that I very deeply wanted my body to be mine. I wanted it desperately, but didn't really know what to do.

Looking at pictures taken when I was twelve, thirteen, and fourteen years old, it's easy to see I was sad. I looked sad and melancholy. I was carrying a kind of heaviness. Something made me feel heavy but I really didn't know what it was or where it came from. But at the time I had to carry it, and when I look back at the pictures I can see it on my young face: I was made heavy by sadness, melancholy and depression; I looked like I was bending under an invisible weight.

Years later, and thanks to my beloved Taoist Master, Grandmaster Mantak Chia, I know that some other spirit was in my body. Strange, not to have my own spirit in my own body! Yet it happens when the mind is not connected to the body. So many negative emotions can enter the inner space of the being but we won't know it's happening if we are not conscious. We'll just feel very badly and have no tools to change it. Some people develop negative thoughts and belief systems, because they carry negativity, like deep sadness in their bodies and this negativity draws them into the depths of apathy. Apathy is one of the most difficult things to overcome and it's caused by sadness. It's the slimy glue of inaction. And yes, this is how many people develop regrets and resentment, and sadly, it sometimes leads to suicide.

People in this state just point their fingers at the world and begin to slowly think that the outer world doesn't like them, that they are not adapted to it and that they have to leave it to find beauty and deep satisfaction. This is what happened to the Romantics in the 19th century: they were a group of people suffering from depression and sorrow, and in some cases, tuberculosis. They are a good example of how negative thoughts and emotions can influence the body. This is exactly the opposite feeling of being satisfied and happy in the here and now.

Instead of searching for the reason of our illnesses outside ourselves, we just have to look inside and change our minds and belief systems. In fact, I discovered that this syndrome is very, very common. I also discovered how to change these feelings within myself and I will tell you later how I did it.

I had to learn that the body is connected to the mind and you can see the workings of the mind by studying the body. The mind is located in each microscopic cell of the body. Each one of our cells is a microcosm of our thoughts. When you begin to practice conscious physical exercise, your body changes: you are rejuvenated because you clear your mind, you concentrate on the physical, you breathe fresh air, breathe in more oxygen and breathe more carbon dioxide out. You clean out your lungs, you develop courage, and you become a little bit more yourself! Why? Because, you need energy to realize your potential and surpass your limitations. You begin to concentrate your primordial essence within yourself to give yourself a chance to grow. You become radiant, full of inner power. You are much nearer to yourself. And this is the beginning of inner consciousness and oneness with your primordial force.

This is the pure primordial life force that causes plants to grow, nature to bloom and seasons to follow each other. This is the root of the pure law of eternal change and movement within nature. This by itself contains natural wisdom. In my life, I've had the opportunity to learn a lot about it without first knowing that it was so important to my spiritual development.

Because my own mind was not connected to my own body as I told you before, I was also not sexually attractive. Young men would never, never choose me as their girlfriend, as their lover. They would just want me as a good friend, as their confidante. I suffered a lot from this. I loved in silence and it broke my heart. I developed a high sense for self sacrifice and because of my sexual energy, my deep physical consciousness was disconnected from my mind. I accepted this terrible rule that made me artificially proud on the outside but terribly sad on the inside. And as I began to have sexual relationships with men, I went on being a victim and even an object of abuse for men who liked it.

But of course, I was the only one who was responsible for that.

As chance would have it, I had a very bad skiing accident at the age of fifteen. I could have died, but no, I just broke my right heel. I discovered that heels carry the weight not only of the body, but also the mind. I had to change my vision of myself to be able to walk again: I had to make myself lighter. Western Medicine condemned me to not walk normally again. But because I was so young and my inner power and creativity were still strong and powerful (even if I didn't know anything about it), I began to feel that life force would be the strongest and I decided to put my mind into my healing. My body went through a terrible shock, as if the universe had slapped me hard enough to kill me. In fact yes, it killed my unconsciousness and made me conscious. It woke me up! I did not experience physical death, but psychological death. That was another sign of body-mind connection: I could not walk anymore but my mind did not want to die. That was the beginning of a very deep transformation that made me walk the walk…step by step, to recover my foot.

What I really want to share with you in this story is the tremendous healing power of Inner Feeling. We really have to feel ourselves to be able to know what we need to transform. Many people are unable to say what they really feel. Sometimes they even resist their feelings because they are afraid of feeling pain. That's why I love one of the main Taoist meditations called "the Inner Smile": it's a really good exercise where you train yourself to be able to smile to every part of your body. And this is exactly how you begin to know that you have pain somewhere, for example, that you have repressed anger hidden in your liver. And so you can transform it because you first train yourself to feel it and to look at it in a smiling, accepting way.

My physical rehabilitation helped me to gradually, but completely, change my mind about myself. Every day I learned to transfer more and more body weight to my injured foot to rehabilitate the bones. It needed a lot of mindful connections to my bone cells and I began to concentrate the most positive energy I could. I smiled to the pain and concentrated my positive, confident, thoughts deep into the bones to help my foot structure rebuild and my bone cells to regenerate. It took months, years to for it to heal completely. But one day, it was there: I could walk again, even spring, dance, ski and climb. I am very proud of it because I did it by myself and it gave my dignity back to me. What a joy, what happiness in my heart. I discovered real love: the ability to love myself. And the most powerful thing is that not only a physical healing process took place but also a psychological one. I was twenty-one and born again.

This is how I discovered the free flow of natural forces within myself and began my Taoist and martial arts training. I would get through. More than that, I would live with complete body and mind and with full joy and happiness. Because I had been able to rebuild my foot, why wouldn't I be able to transform my whole being into a little pearl of life force? It was just a matter of self-confidence and deep trust in the healing process I had discovered.

Year after year, I went on being a passionate lover of nature. I began to teach others to find the path to oneness; to Mother Earth and Universal Forces. I felt the flow of living life force more and more, and went on teaching and studying energy work, Tai Chi Chuan, Martial Arts (Shaolin Kung Fu) and Aikido. I went on searching for this treasure that interconnects the mind, the breath and the movement because my intuition told me to go that way. I was completely dedicated to the process of rebuilding, strengthening and refining my inner structure.

Once, as I was training with Master Chia on the Tai Chi field at Tao Garden, I had a kind of vision that still guides me today when I get lost: I saw myself on a kind of Path of Life holding the Iron Shirt Posture of the Tree, which is one of the main standing meditation trainings in energy work: you learn how to calm your mind and your heart down to make yourself physically strong and smooth and to connect yourself with the

Primordial Force. From this moment on, I knew that my whole life would always be connected to this force, that I could feel guided and supported even in the most terrible and painful moments: I completely opened my heart to knowledge and wisdom, I talked secretly to myself and said: Okay, let's go for it!

It still resonates in my heart cells…

2nd part: Let's go for it!

We all know that vital energy is all about love, isn't it? How can we progress if we don't feel a deep love for what we study, for a beautiful movement, for the work itself that brings you back to yourself and makes your soul feel so happy? Love heals and gives faith in everything. Love is magic, and it pushes you forward.

My favorite trainings are the traditional Saber and Sword Tai Ji forms. The movement takes me deep within myself. I can experience inner strength and beauty, simplicity and combativeness at the same time. But to be able to feel this pure joy I have to dedicate my whole heart to hours of training per week, and I am used to training in any weather – wind, snow, heat or rain – to maintain deep integrity and to feel oneness with nature, stabilizing my body inner temperature.

When I started learning this path, I mixed up a few things and instead of concentrating my heart on its connections to the mind and lower energy Centers, I dispersed its force sometimes at falling in love with my teachers because I admired their knowledge. And I just loved them too much.

In this chapter, consider that men are like fire and women are like water. Each element is balanced by traces of its opposite. When fire touches water, what happens? Water becomes steam … and this is actually what love is and where sexual fusion of the two partners occurs.

The alchemy of fire and water needs to be regulated, of course: if passion is too strong, fire devastates the valley. When men's fire and women's fire cannot find balance in their relationships, it can burn out of control, creating fire emotions like anger, jealousy, excess possessiveness and violence. Conversely, if water extinguishes fire, what happens? Water emotions like fear, lack of self confidence, anxiety or boredom can occur. Love without fire doesn't sound so good, does it? This is the lack of love: water stays too cold, there is no pleasure, and this can just lead to neurosis.

Do you understand how love works on a pure energetic level? It follows the pure natural flow; water and fire have just to be balanced to bring the couple to steam… and pure joy occurs.

The problem is that at the beginning of my real "Love Initiation" I was so passionate and mixing my heart connection to the Tai Ji (which was regulating myself) with the heart connection I thought I had to my male teachers (which was completely taking me out of balance). In fact it's a very common mistake to let your teacher be your lover. While their hearts weren't mine, the presence of their masculine fire, in addition to all the fire I was putting into our connection, was too much for my feminine, watery emotions. It was not taking me to emotional balance. I felt pressured and forced. My feminine self was still feeling abused and poor; I felt as if I was never strong enough. I dispersed my own fire, gave too much, spent too much energy and money and got finally in real trouble on my own personal path… I discovered that my fire and water were completely out of balance. I knew that was not the way, but I had to learn concretely how to regulate my own fire and water. I had to calm my fire down and make it be wiser, and I had to strengthen my water; make it become self-confident.

This alchemical process was revealed to me step by step. Only experimentation could teach this to me and it took me time to be able to really adjust my elements, but my life experiences had enhanced my willpower. This was one of the positive things about my water element. I had a lot of endurance and I was very persevering. It made me be a courageous girl. At that time, I very, very slowly began to move past my victimhood.

Now I would say that love has to be learned and trained, experimented with. In martial arts, we learn how to adjust facing our partners on the tatami, but we never learn how to love…

A loving and balanced relationship is the result of the personal path of both woman and man and reflects their wisdom; the work they performed on themselves to balance their water and fire. Love is a jewel of secret alchemy.

Dear Reader, I told you all this to let you slowly, slowly go to the secret of my subject, which is the key of my inner realization.

I was searching for something and … I found it. Love became my Master. I understood that I had been able to repair my foot because I had learned to love my body. Cell after cell I had re-learned to love it and to send so much love to my bones, that not only was my foot repaired, but my body also became beautiful and my sexual energy blossomed like a flower. I found that each time I went somewhere I could meet new men and have new sexual experiences. My intention had reached my body. I was just a woman who changed her mind. My thoughts could influence my body. If I wanted to be something, I just had to smile to my body and dream of it. After a while, it happened. I noticed in my happy heart that I was rejuvenating, that one could read my happiness on my face and body. I was discovering the art of mastering myself.

My life became like a bunch of flowers. My heart was blossoming and shining inner joy and satisfaction, and I could fall in love and be loved. I began to like it so much that it became a game to have lovers, many of them in the same time and many different, even men who had girlfriends or were married. I began to take risks, to open my heart more and more, to embrace every chance (I thought!) that was given to me as an experience and I liked it so much because it was flattering my ego, that I could not stop anymore. I was like a little, immature girl playing with a new toy.

If you consider that love is fire and fire is located in the heart, my heart was burning. I had a forest fire in my chest and brain. I went to the extreme point of what I could give and disperse, to the total expansion of my fire of that time. And because it was extreme, I also began to lose vital energy. My sexual energy and heart were disconnecting again.

Because I have a good heart, I am also very sincere, enthusiastic, and courageous. I am always ready to learn, to respect the source of the living teachings I receive, and to grow the good. And because I knew that our life experiences and our romantic situations are just reflecting what we are and what we think, I just decided to change myself again and to correct what was going wrong.

I really feel that we human beings have the potential to look sincerely inside, smile to ourselves, recognize problems, accept them, and change them. If we want to change our minds, we first have to get some distance from our emotional reactions, to come down into our little "inner laboratory" and change the ingredients of the magical formula. We are able to do that. It requires full consciousness, calmness and a clear intent, and…a small drop of willpower. You do that, you become a fairy. You can change yourself and master your emotions.

My astrological chart is very clear about the fact that I was born with a very weak Water Element. Even my Qi Gong Master advised me once to settle down on an island. "You need to live surrounded by water," he said, "You need it to be balanced and happy, and in good health." The further I got into myself, the more I could clearly read into the manifestations of this apparent little fact. Fire was taking my mind out of balance and no water could stop it. If you consider that water is controlling very specific organs in your body, you've got the key. That's exactly what I did. "Use your tools!", said the little voice of the fairy. "Use your tools!" And I disappeared into the beautiful blue sea.

3rd part: Whaoooooooh how magic life is!

At that period of my life, I was living on a beach near Montpellier on the French south coast. And one day, looking at the beach and the sea, I could see something I had not noticed before. I could see a girl dressed with a swimming costume, a blue, white and red wetsuit, and holding flippers in her hand walking along the beach where the waves were breaking. "That must be a lifesaver", I said to myself. I ran downstairs to the beach to meet her. I was a little bit intimidated by the presence of the lifeguards, so I hid myself for a while and waited until I could meet the girl along the beach. "Hello! You have a great job! Could you tell me what I have to do to become one of you?", I shyly asked. "Yes, sure," she said, with a big smile, and began to tell me more about the way to become a marine lifesaver on the French coast. I thanked her sincerely and flew back to my temple.

I loved swimming and I used to run every day. I was trained to exercise outside in any weather. My heart was so happy and I discovered there was a job that could fit very well with my wild and sportive nature, and open myself to further communication with people I would never have met another way. Lifesaving in the ocean had been a dream. I mustered all my courage and forces and prepared myself physically and psychologically for the difficult tests I had in front of me.

I tell you, dear reader, never, ever give up your dreams. Always go further into the realization of your dream. The heart is the organ that controls the realization of your dreams. Follow your heart, fill it with joy, and light and listen to it sincerely. It will show you the path.

I made it, I got it, and I became a lifeguard. I went through the most intense physical effort I have ever exerted in my life. I rescued many lives, helped a lot of people to get back to the beach, saved my own life, saved my heart, and balanced it with the pure blue ocean's stormy water.

I tell you, dear Reader, never forget to follow your intuition and listen to what you want in the deepest layers of your own being. Stick to your spirit and be yourself.

As the Australian Shaman says: "You think of it, you feel it, you do it!" But you have to do it. Once again it involves training. You focus your intention, your full conscious mind, into your heart and do with happiness something you always dreamed of doing. You will align your mind, your heart and your body. You will feel enlightened and radiate positive energy. Then you will attract positivity from others by doing good things for yourself and you invite others to do the same.

I tell you this because it's the keystone of my romantic sky. Three more initiatory stages followed this main commitment of my life until I was able to meet the man of my life. Because I am a woman of commitment, I practice the commitment to joy. I committed to do good to myself, to heal myself and to love myself. And my heart felt good. I didn't feel forced or humiliated anymore. This was very precious to my heart's health. If I felt badly about any relationship, I knew I had something to correct in myself first. I needed to stay in harmony with what I thought, felt, and did.

As I began to strengthen my water element by spending so many hours a day in water, my heart became supported by my kidneys. They got stronger, very simply strengthened by water. In nature, the kidneys, bladder, sexual organs, bones, and nervous system are controlled by the water element. I had been consciously going back to water and water was healing my body and psyche. How magic life is.

And this is how I repaired my humiliated, wounded heart that had made me react as a victim in the past. My heart got proud and strong, but still sensitive, secure and soft. I didn't cry out in distress anymore. On the contrary. I was the one who saved people from distress by swimming to them, calming them down, and bringing them back to the safe, dry sand. My heart was gently healing and gaining self-confidence. I was in harmony with my inner femininity. I was respecting myself and harnessing the simple secret of growing the good.

The key was that I was feeling secure and began to surely recover my inner strength. My heart was happy and my body was well trained by beautiful and powerful natural elements that made me physically and psychologically feel bliss all over my cells every day.

Some time later, I chose to become a lifesaver on the dangerous beaches of our Atlantic Coast at the seaside resort of Lacanau. Imagine big waves on kilometres of wild sand beaches and sun shining above the ocean – a surfer's paradise. It was quite something for a girl to work there. All my colleagues where big and tall muscular guys. I will always remember consulting the I Ching (the traditional Chinese "Book of Changes") before leaving for two months to work on this beach. I read card 29 which is "Great Danger." I learned a lot about life and death and feminine immortality.

Indeed I was surrounded by macho men collecting feminine conquests every night. I had never seen this. They had different girlfriends every night. Instead of plotting a feminist revenge against those guys, I decided that I had to learn something from this, and that it would be a nice opportunity for me to live in the archetype of the "Feminine Warrior" for a while. It was an enlightening experience. This didn't happen by accident. I had to see love more from the outside, from the Yang masculine part of my consciousness to strengthen my Yin feminine force. And I had the chance to see what it meant to be a victim of the predator like all those inexperienced girls were. And the most interesting thing was that all those girls wanted that and totally let it happen without trying to change anything. It was a kind of law. It was like this: Guys used their Yang, male fire energy to consume Yin feminine fresh water energy. It was all so artificial and disgusting. I used my knowledge to remember that men are Yin, fresh and tender inside and women are Yang, fiery and powerful inside. Why did all those people lose their inner power like this around me? I had promised myself to learn something from all this. And I did.

I noticed that men used their incredible external capacity to disconnect with their emotional worlds and their hearts by denying their Yin, sensitive part. Conversely, girls were just denying their strong Yang inner world to let their outer, emotional and sensitive Yin fall prey to these guys. Something was not right. And, as a girl, I decided to learn from the guys, from what they had that could be helpful to me. Control of their emotions. I did it. I chose three attractive guys I liked the most, loved them and left them before they mentioned any intention. They were completely amazed. No girl had done this to them before. And as a result, they wanted me. They looked for me and desired me. I had made them face their Yin. I was facing my own Yang, my inner force and my capacity not to invest my heart at all, to be able to control my excess of fire. I took risks, but I got the knowledge and I just disappeared and left the dangerous game at the right time I think. I had found the key of keeping Yin and Yang balanced in myself as far as a loving relationship is concerned. I knew that now I would open my heart consciously and carefully to the man and only to the man who would be the one that would do justice to me, as well as I did to myself. And I dove into a kind of inner retreat where I took care of my feminine garden, pampering my flowers, watering them with true love flowing down from my heart, and breathing in their delicate fragrance. I was making myself ready for my prince.

And this is how, months later, I met Benoît. He is my husband and the father of our beautiful child.

You must know that training your body consciously will stimulate your immune and your hormonal system. You develop a lot a sexual energy. You strengthen your kidneys, fortify your bones, and develop an acute mental focus to accomplish your goals. You develop a lot of fire in your physical body that pushes you forward and stimulates your mind to reach your objectives. That will also slow your heart down more and more and you will live longer. If you want to maintain a good level of practice when you age, you have to cool your muscles down, stretch your body diligently, and lubricate your joints with Qi Gong or Tai Chi exercise. These healthy practices will balance your body and eventually extend your sportive life to an advanced age. Your body will allow you to train longer. Your body will keep you as its best friend because it knows you are ready to do well to it and not to make it suffer more. This is exactly what we call giving water to the fire. This is the alchemy of love in everything. And this is also my love secret.

I trained for years in water because I love swimming and bodysurfing in the ocean's waves and my body is in harmony with my heart. I train Qi Gong, Tai Chi and Taoist Inner Alchemy every day. I swim and run and dance. My mind, my heart, and my body are happy together. They are all good friends. The atmosphere is good at home. Consider that your body is pure water where everything is flowing smoothly and melting with your heart joy that radiates heat and tenderness to all of your cells. Add the most beautiful sunrises on the ocean, mixing with the white magic foam of the waves rolling to the beach. How can you be unhappy in that kind of state? This is harmony with nature, harmony of a peaceful mind, heart and action. And this is what I have felt in my daily practice now for years.

This kind of energy free-flow helped me tremendously to repair my wounded heart and help to deal with my emotions. Since I decided to be myself, love myself, and be good to myself by having the natural life I was dreaming of, I was able to attract the man of my life.

I am not serious. I am just a woman who realizes her dreams.

Fabienne Pignard-Marthod

New Caledonia, April 2009

Chapter 7

Couple Personality Types

The minute I heard my first love story I started looking for you, not knowing how blind that was. Lovers don't finally meet somewhere. They're in each other all along.

-Rumi

In book One, we looked at some of the wacky personality types you could run into when dating. No way to name them all, but we had fun.

Now that you have graduated to the wonderful world of Commitment, we have Couple Personality Types to play with. Of course, you and your partner may fluctuate in and out of any number of these personas on the zany roller coaster ride of romantic couple-dom. I had to pick just a few, so read on with an open mind and see how many of these apply to you or people you know.

Just like book #1, Why Real Women Drink Straight Tequila - The Tao of Intimacy, there is a story woven through these to help make this a bit more entertaining.

Yours in the Tao,

Sarina

Nesters

Nest

1. The community of animals living in a nest

2. A cozy, protected, or secluded place

3. To make or live in a nest, especially in preparation for giving birth to young

4. To make a place more comfortable and homelike (informal)

Encarta® World English Dictionary © 1999 Microsoft Corporation. All rights reserved. Developed for Microsoft by Bloomsbury Publishing Plc.

"At the center of your being you have the answer; you know who you are and you know what you want."

-Laozi

Here's a twist on an old joke:

Q. What does a Nester bring on the second date?

A. A moving van.

Nesters are people whose main focus is to create a home with another person. Who that person is tends to be damned near irrelevant in the choosing process; many figure out if this was a good idea later.

Your classic Nesters are extremely comfortable in your home right away – and rightly so, they are about to move in. They conveniently "forget" their toothbrushes in your bathroom after the second time they have a sleep over. You can nudge them in the morning and say, "Hey, I have to go to work," and they will groggily respond "OK honey, see you when you get home."

Shocking, but it happens every day.

Now, if you have a strong spine, you will invite them to get the hell up, rinse off, and get the hell out. You may even feel a trickle of perspiration roll down your face as you lock that door behind the both of you on your way out.

But, if you are a sweetie and just can't bear to hurt their feelings, you may just have a five-course meal waiting for you after work. Your plants will be watered, your laundry clean, dry, and folded. A Nester can be magnificent at showing you how much better life is together.

What if the Nester wants you to move in?

If a Nester owns a home and wants you to move in, they will make you a key, start calling things "ours", and definitely won't kick you out when they leave for work. No, you will probably wake to fresh coffee and a little love note.

I'm not saying this is good, or bad. I'm just saying, "lover, beware".

Classically, Nesters are women. Actually, the joke above was originally a lesbian joke. And truth be told, the funniest stories I've heard about lovers moving in straight away are about lesbian couples. I hate to say it, but some of my favorite women are Nesters and the drive to find a partner can be really insane.

The stories I hear about men who initiate cohabitating right away tend to be related to a sincere need to move or the need to share bills. Not very romantic, unless…

Both people are Nesters! Yes, Nesters should partner with other Nesters!

Why not? If both people are into living together and sharing their lives, it could work. Wherein this would be preposterous for a Lone Wolf, to a Nester this is just good sense.

Both parties should want a live-in lover and a companion at home. They can figure out if this was an intelligent move later.

...and if it doesn't work out, our lovable Nesters will hit the pavement and find new birds.

Why Real Couples Drink Straight Tequila - A Love Story

by Sarina Stone

I had a dream last night. I was watching myself in a life that looked just like mine...

Part 1

"Organic decaf mixed with soy, please."

"Yes ma'am."

When did I become a ma'am? Got to get back to the gym. What time is it? 8:45? Shit! Late again. Jacob's going to kill me. No, he's used to it. So are my listeners. What? Coffee's ready? Cool, I gotta run.

"Thank you. See you tomorrow," I said to the cashier after I paid.

And with that, I grabbed a lid for my decaf, honey, and soy latte and stuffed it in my purse, turned around, and slammed right in to the guy standing in line behind me. Thank goodness the coffee only spilled on me, leaving his very expensive but casual clothes bone dry.
Okay, no problem, so I have a little coffee on my t-shirt. No one but Jacob and the crew will see it. Besides, I have that brand new little Jil Sander jacket in the back seat. I've been dying to show it off.

"Oh, God. I'm so sorry." I said.

"No problem. Looks like you got the worst of it." He said. "Gary. Gary Parker."

And with that Gary Parker extended his amazingly well -manicured hand in greeting.
"Nice to meet you, Gary," I said as I extended my hand and shook his. I looked up in to his eyes and instantly, there was electricity. This was bad - very bad.

Gary was over six feet tall, had thick brown hair and an air of

understated sophisticat on. He was fabulous, friendly, and spoke with clarity. I
desperately needed to ignore him.

You know how every once in a while you meet strangers and feel like you know them? And if they feel the same way about you, most of the time you end up having this mysterious bond that goes beyond logic? When I looked in to Gary Parker's eyes, I felt like asking him if we knew each other. I felt at home and freaked out all at once. Yes, he was gorgeous, but it was more than that. I know he felt it too, because he introduced himself and then just stared at me.

Gary stared at me so long it got weird - probably because he was still shaking my hand. Actually, he stopped shaking my hand and just sort of held it.

"Umm, I'd like to take that with me, Gary," I said, looking at our joined hands.

"Oh. Yeah," he said, letting go. "Sorry about that. Do I know you?"

"I don't know, and I'm late," I said. "Sorry about the crash. Glad I didn't ruin your shirt. It looks like it was made for you."
"It was," said stud boy, I mean Gary, as I made myself look away and head for the door.

Just get in the car, Sarina, just get in the car and start driving.

8:55am.

'It looks like it was made for you.' Ugh. Why do stupid things fall out of my mouth when I meet a hot guy? Where do all the smart words go in these situations? Why does my intelligence and saliva just dry up if I'm attracted to someone? I'm such a freak.

Focus, Sarina.

I parked the car. No problem. I can do this. It is still five minutes before we go live. I jumped out and put the fabulous jacket on to cover the coffee. Buttoned up like a good conservative businesswoman, I grabbed my purse, the coffee (what was left of it), and the brief case. Excellent. Shut the door, hit the lock, and we're off.

RIP!

Oh, heck no! You did not just do what I think you did, Stone. A piece of my brand new Jil Sander jacket was hanging out of the car door. It got caught when I shut the door and was now hanging in shreds not only from the door, but on me as well. Two of the four buttons were gone from the front and somehow the lightweight fabric had ripped wide open, up the back, almost up to the shoulder. One more casualty of the Sarina-getting-to-work-on-time war.

As luck would have it, the fricking elevator was being repaired (I swear to God), and I ended up running up eight flights of stairs to get to the studio. By the time I got in there, it was 9:01, I had a ripped jacket, a coffee stained t-shirt, and was panting out of breath (yet, another reason to hit the gym).

I bolted into the studio, ignoring the "on air" sign, grabbed my headset, and plunked down just in time to say, "Welcome to Couple Chat. On cue - I'm Sarina Stone."

And with that, I settled in my chair and into my gentle, soothing, professional voice, and got ready to dish dating advice to my lovelorn listeners.

Future Mothers & Fathers of the World

Future

1. Time that has yet to come

2. Events that have not yet happened

3. An expected or projected state

Encarta® World English Dictionary © 1999 Microsoft Corporation. All rights reserved. Developed for Microsoft by Bloomsbury Publishing Plc.

Your task is not to seek for love, but merely to seek and find all the barriers within yourself that you have built against it.

-Rumi

The following Personality Type is one the educated adult is painfully aware of. As much as I hate to mention the elephant in the room, I'm going to because there may be some young person out there who is hearing this concept for the first time.

OR

Perhaps some of you more seasoned lovers need a gentle reminder.

How many times have you heard someone say, "I will NEVER be like my mother," or "I will NEVER be like my father," then five minutes later they holler at you for drinking milk out of the container? Actually, I hate that, too. Ok, so they holler at you for leaving dirty socks on the floor. No, wait, that's gross, you deserved that one. Let's say they reprimand you for neglecting to finish your dinner (well, I slaved over a hot stove and this is the thanks I get?).

Umm, I need a moment. Sigh.

Were your parents slobs? Did they yell at each other? Did one of them have affairs? Was there alcoholism or messy divorce? Ignore each other or you?

If you answered yes to any of these, keep yourself in check. We see two types of long-term responses from kids who lived with "normal" dysfunction. a) They grow up to emulate the dysfunction, or b) They grow up dramatically on the other side of the dysfunction (i.e. if your folks were slobs, you may be a neat freak).

Most of us continue to play out the roles we saw as youths – especially the roles of the people who raised us. Those unfortunate souls who were raised in severe dysfunction or abuse may actually have a leg up on the rest of us who think their childhood was normal. A victim of an obviously poor upbringing is more apt to seek council and de-program the dysfunction. With help, they may actually erase the need to keep repeating their pasts and instead, rewrite self-chosen destinies.

It's the rest of us who think their folks were a little wacky, but see no need to dwell, who end up right back where we started: Future Mothers & Fathers of the World.

Now this can be really icky sometimes. For example, using alcoholics tend to partner with people who will tolerate their alcoholism. Often, though not always, the co-dependant partner has experienced a level of love with an addict previously. It's not so weird when you understand that these two people are just playing out roles. So, the alcoholic gets to be pampered and saved, and the co-dependant gets to cover up and make excuses; just like they always knew it would be.

On the lighter side of this issue, we have people who are attracted to dear old mom or a guy just like daddy, and it works. Yes, the Future Mothers & Fathers of the World can pair off in a healthy, functional way if that which attracts them is love. You see, all that stuff we saw as kids and blew off as a little wacky can actually be endearing if it isn't running some subliminal, self-sabotaging program in our brains. Why not be attracted to the most awesome quality in your dad or mom? How about creating a loving relationship with someone who inspires you to repeat the cool things your family represented when you were a tot? People do it every day and I'm telling you it works.

Yes, Future Mothers & Fathers of the World, it's ok to unite if it is done with mindfulness and love. Conscious emulation of the best of our parents is a wonderful aspiration and will surely contribute to health and happiness in your partnership.

Part 2

I host a funky radio show called Couple Chat. Together with thousands around the world who take responsibility for their romantic destinies, I represent The Quantum Dating Club. I'm sort of the hub and I invite speakers, writers, and fans to connect via the show, books, and various social media.

Against all odds, I have a huge following. The show is recorded live in the warehouse district of Minneapolis, Minnesota, and is headed for syndication. Some days I take calls and other days I roll interviews.

The platform is simple: me and a few other advisors offer advice based on the Chinese philosophy of Taoism and its relationship to the realms of romantic intimacy and commitment. On the show, we use Taoist principals to predict or guide the romantic destinies of our listeners. By advising callers to take actions that shift the balance of certain emotional elements, we enable them to improve their circumstances at the root of their dysfunctions and become balancing factors in their own lives. This may sound complicated, but it's not. The callers on the other hand…So, The Quantum Dating Club's advice to the lovelorn is unique since most people don't even know what the word Tao means, and even fewer are familiar with the principals contained therein.

"Our first caller is Robert from Saint Paul. Go ahead Robert, let's chat," I said exactly the same way I say it every day. I'm a pro.

"My girlfriend is freaking me out," said Robert from Saint Paul.

"How so, Bob?" I said, "Can I call you Bob?"

"I wish you wouldn't," Robert replied. "Only my mom calls me Bob.

That's a long story."

"No problem, Robert," I said. "What's your question, sweetie?"

"Well, like I said, my girlfriend is freaking me out. We've been dating for about 6 weeks and the other day she tells me she doesn't want to use birth control."

My eyes rolled so far back I was concerned they would get stuck in my head.

"Ummm," I said. "And just how did she present this brilliant idea to you?"

"I was saying that, since we were in a monogamous relationship, maybe we should come up with a more comfortable form of birth control than condoms."

"Sounds reasonable," I chimed in.

"Yeah, I thought so, too. I mean, don't get me wrong, I'm a little weirded out right now, but I'm really in to this woman. She's amazing. She could be the one. I want birth control that's a little less, uh, latex. I figured we'd just get tested, choose some pill or IUD and throw the condoms away.

Anyhow, she says 'Why use anything?' and I said, 'I'm thinking the obvious answer is to prevent pregnancy.' And the next thing you know, she's telling me she doesn't want to use anything because she wants to have my love child and know me forever."

At this point my producer dramatically put both hands over his face and pretended to wrestle with what ever was about to come out of his mouth.

I collected myself.

"Robert, let me ask you some questions. Did you say you've been together six weeks?"

"Yeah."

"Is she gorgeous, available, sexy? Make you laugh?"

"Yeah."

"Best lover you ever had? The creative type?"

"You have no idea."

"Okay, stay with me. She says you're her soul mate, and that she's never felt like this before?"

"Yeah man," Robert said, "just like that."

I picked up the pace from there. "Robert?"

"Yeah?"

"Did she tell you all of this within the first three dates?"

A pin-drop silence.

"Yes," he said finally. His response was whisper soft, but the message was loud and clear. We had hit home.

"She totally gets you. And the miracle is – she likes all the same stuff you do. It's uncanny. It's like you've known each other forever."

"Yeah," said Robert from Saint Paul, sort of breathy and low. "How'd you know?"

My producer flashed me a knowing look and pointed at me to take it from there.

"Robert," I said, "I think we've spotted your girlfriend's Personality

Type. We know what's going to happen if you don't figure out who you're dealing with."

"What the heck are you talking about?" Robert said.

"She's a Fantasy Addict!" I shouted into the microphone and almost blew my eardrum out. "This gal is classic. Bring out your Tao of Intimacy book and read the section on Fantasy Addicts.

You go on vacation with Fantasy Addicts, but you don't actually take them seriously. Holy shit. Love child? How many guys has she said that to? Dude, are you crazy?"

"Yeah?" said Robert meekly.

My producer was losing his mind. Sometimes I forget myself and swear on the air.

"Alright," I said, "let's tone it back a notch. Robert?"

"Yeah?"

"You know how forest fires burn really hot, fast and wild?"

"Yeah."

"This gal is like one of those fires. I know you can't see it right now, but she's burning too hot to maintain this velocity. She's going to burn out. And when she does, things are going to change. It's probably not a great time to make a baby together. Know what I mean?"

"Not really."

"Okay, just tell her she needs to use birth control. And if the two of you still want to make a baby in 6 months, you can re-visit the topic. Okay?"

"Yeah. Wait. Are you saying this isn't going to last?"

I took a deep breath. "If she doesn't calm the fire down to a burning ember and just act normal. If she doesn't show you who she really is, she won't be able to keep up the 'I'm so independent and cool façade' forever and yeah, those Fiery Fantasy relationships can end pretty quickly and abruptly. A nice glowing ember burns much longer and with far less tending. But, hey... whoever loved that loved not at first sight? This may indeed be the love of your life; call us back in six or eight months and we'll talk again. In the meantime, take initiative and wear your hat to the party. Okay?"

"Okay. I feel really weird now," said Robert.

"Good. Your eyes are opening. Sometimes the initial shock of light is uncomfortable. Call us back with an update. Thanks for calling, Robert." I said. "We're going to take a break and enjoy the musical style of the lovely Miss Billy Holiday. When we return, we have a caller who is angry with her boyfriend for being lousy with money."

"We're clear for four minutes," came the voice from the control room.

Part 3

In case you don't know yet, Taoism or the Tao is a philosophy, not a religion. It assumes there is a natural connection between pretty much everything. If you don't like the whole Eastern philosophy thing (yeah, this philosophy originated in China, so Tao is a Chinese word), then look at science. Quantum Manifesting holds many of the same principals and has many levels of understanding. For example, there is a connection between humans simply because we are all made of the same stuff. And this stuff is completely interrelated. On a Quantum level, it makes sense because the word Quantum can refer to the smallest possible unit needed to connect two or more things. According to the Tao, or The Way of Nature, we see that we are also connected simply because we are conscious, energetic creatures Same conclusion, but a different path to get there.

To go deeper, each person emulates and is connected with elements of nature. The body and mind each have uncanny connections to nature and various aspects of it. The heart really is the home of fire, love, and hate, as the kidneys are the home of water, gentleness, and fear. Crazy as it seems, I can predict the actions of certain Personality Types based on which element they are emulating at the moment. My producer, Jacob, and I do it all the time and it's making us famous. But really, we're just really good at paying attention to detail.

Anyhow, simply put, the level of balance between elemental energies within an individual is in direct proportion to that individual's physical and mental state.

Consider the element of fire:

The Fire Element corresponds to summer. This is the time of greatest warmth and light, the longest days, the greatest activity and luxuriant growth. In the individual Fire correspondences include the ability to establish relationships, express love and sexuality, expansiveness, enthusiasm, passion, playfulness, joyfulness, warmth and relaxation. The organ systems include the heart, small intestine, pericardium, and sympathetic and parasympathetic nervous systems. When the Fire Element is not in balance there is a lack of joy and warmth, difficulty in intimate relationships, depression, confusion and doubt, low energy, digestive problems such as irritable bowel syndrome, insomnia, cardiac disease, and tinnitus.[1]

Now, there's an element we don't want burning out of control! A flame that burns too hot will eventually burn out. They always do, you can set your watch by it. However, a nice glowing ember, with a little fuel and care, can go on and on for quite some time. Apply this theory to romance and we can predict, with eerie accuracy, which guys or gals will dump their partners within the first few months because they will simply burn out and lose interest.

1   From http://www.southwestnutrition.com/chinese.html

Remember the Fantasy Addict Personality Type from Why Real Women Drink Straight Tequila – The Tao of Intimacy? They always come on like an out-of-control forest fire. In other words, they start with an unreasonably high burning flame that requires an outrageous amount of fuel, or energy, to maintain. Now, we made a bit of fun of that Personality Type, and if you understand the element of Fire, you would see that this obsessive passion could not possibly remain over the long haul. Eventually, they run out of fuel and burn out. It's only funny if you see it coming. If you take this Personality Type seriously, you get to be disappointed and probably broken hearted when they disappear.

Even if they partner with a strong Water element, necessary to balance the Fire, too much Fire still tends to dry up the Water over time. If the more passive lover isn't careful, they may end up emotionally depleted or fried. Meanwhile, our high burning flame will refuel and search for a new conquest to frizzle up until they, once again, burn out. Not that they are vicious; they are simply puppets to their unconscious patterns. As a life coach, I respect and serve the Victims and the Persecutors because so often it's hard to tell who's playing which role. When we understand the relationship between the elements, and ourselves, we clearly see the predictability of our outcomes.

I have seen this so many times that I no longer doubt that this Tao is very real, and understanding the Way of Nature makes my little radio show one of a kind in the romance industry. You may even be reading this story in one of my books right now - another dream of mine.

"You look like hell," said Eric, sussing me up.

"Bite me," I delicately replied. "And nice to see you. Thanks for coming. People love you in this town."

"And quoting Christopher Marlow? Come on, TaoLady. Run out of Laozi and Rumi quotes?"

"Not at all," I said. "I just thought it was apropos. People do meet, fall in love, and stay that way sometimes, you know."

Eric Thurnbeck was years younger than me, but was a brilliant psychic consultant and a counselor. No romantic relations here; we both like men. He had flown in for a couple of weeks to do the show with me and I was relieved. We were relaxed with each other and it was always an exciting show when the two of us worked together. Sometimes Eric was my voice of reason.

"Really, is that how it's working out for you and Brad?" he snickered.

"Brad? You mean Mr. I Need Attention 24/7?

Let me tell you about Brad. Brad is why I was late this morning. Brad is why I'm late all the time. The guy has no respect for my career or my personal space. I can't even brush my teeth with him coming up behind me and doing the little Bradley dance."

"Oh, poor baby," he cooed as he leaned forward and lightly wiggled my right ear.

"You're on in five, four, three.. " came the voice from the control room.
"Welcome back to Couple Chat. I'm Sarina Stone…"

"And I'm Eric Thurnbeck."

I launched right in. "Our second caller is Jennifer from Minneapolis. She says she's sick and tired of her boyfriends' reckless behavior around money. Actually, she was a bit less tactful – I'm paraphrasing. Go ahead Jennifer, let's chat."

"My boyfriend, Donald, is the worst money manager in the world. He makes money, but he spends it all. I just found out he's been hiding debts from me, too. I just don't think I can take it. I mean, I don't want to go down with the ship, you know?"

"Does he hit you?" I asked.

"Oh. God no," said Jennifer.

"Does he verbally abuse you?" I asked.

"Definitely not," she answered.

"Is he cheating on you?" I asked.

"Never," she said.

"Does he make you laugh?"

"Every day," said Jennifer.

"Does he hold you when the world is overwhelming and tell you everything is going to be okay?"

"Yes," she said with a lot less fire in her voice.

I started staring at my hands again. Sometimes the J.O.B. runs smack into my personal life. It can be an occupational hazard when dishing dating advice. Some days I hate having to listen to myself say the healthy stuff when I know I'm not doing it at home. We teach that which we need to learn.

"Then, if I were you," I said, "I'd sit down with him and talk this out. It sounds like you're good with money and he's not. Am I correct?"

"Yes."

"Then see if he would be open to letting you handle the money while he can handle something else, like getting better at his job or fixing up your house. Figure out what he's good at and help him to grow the positive."

"What does he do for a living?" Eric asked. I jumped. I had forgotten he was even there.

"He's a massage therapist." She said. "But that's just to earn his way through school. He's studying to become an architect."

I could hear the adoration in her voice now.

"Jennifer, this guy sounds like a wonderful life partner. Architects bring a lot to the table both financially and artistically."

"What do you mean artistically?" she asked.

"I mean, there's more to success than money, sweetheart."

"Absolutely," she beamed.

Then Eric chimed in, "What are you going to do if he turns out to be a happy millionaire who still can't balance a check book?"

Jennifer didn't answer. So I helped her out.

"I'll tell you exactly what she's going to do, Eric. She's gonna convince her boyfriend to give his earnings to a terrific, trustworthy accountant. She's going to help that accountant save or invest what they can. She's going to do the job that her man can't do because she knows she's in a partnership and partners support each other into a better life."

"Really?" Eric said suddenly. "Is that what a good partner's supposed to do?"

"Yes, that's exactly what a part..." And then I got it. I sat there for a couple seconds, because he was staring at me with this look in his eyes that said he wasn't talking about Jennifer anymore. Eric had done what Eric always does, snuck in under the radar, and hit me dead center.
"Are you implying Jennifer's not a good partner?"

"No. All I'm saying is that you just gave her great advice. Jennifer should listen to it."

"Uh- huh."

"Sounds like Donald is a great guy. That's all I'm saying."

"Uh- huh," I said again. "Maybe Donald should give Jennifer her space!"

"Umm, guys?" Jennifer chimed in, "I'm actually ok with Donald in my space. We're fine there. I just called about the money thing."

I gave Eric the evil eye for a few seconds and then leaned into the microphone. Boy was I pissed, but you wouldn't know it by the sweet tone of my voice. Sugar ants were pouring out of my mouth.

"Jenn, you already know what you need to do about the money issues. Once you get on track with this, everything's going to be just peachy. But you need to grow the good tonight. So, when your man gets home, I want you to think about why you fell in love with him, and share that attitude of gratitude. I want you make passionate love to that man and tell him how grateful you are that he's in your life."

"Besides," Eric added, "that'll make the 'accountant' pill slide down much easier."

"That's right," I said. "We catch more flies with honey. So, Jenn, you feel like you know what you need to do?"

"Yes ma'am!" said Jennifer and promptly hung up.

"Jennifer just got introduced to a part of herself she forgot she had. She remembered that she is a great girlfriend who loves and respects her man."

Eric leaned into his microphone. "Jenn, if you can hear us, please call back in a few weeks and tell us how it's going."

I nodded my head. Once again, not a really good habit for a radio personality.

"For the rest of you out there," crooned Eric, "how about a little Mazzy Star and Dean Martin to finish up our first hour at work?" "Enjoy, enjoy."

"We're off. You guys have 10 minutes and 45 seconds. You'll have two minutes to wrap up when we come back," came the voice from the control room.

I returned to staring at my hands to avoid tearing.

"Well, that was interesting," Eric said.

"Yeah," I retorted.

"What'd I do? All I was saying is that Jennifer should respect her partner."

"Oh, bullshit. We both know who you were talking about."

"Really?"

"Look, all I'm saying is that Brad's too high maintenance. You're not there, you don't see it. I mean, the other day, we were sitting in the same room, and I was working on my laptop. He starts staring at me. I can feel it even though I'm busy. Then walks over to me, kneels down, looks up and says 'I'm jealous of your work.' I think I just stared at him because I wanted to scream 'Then get a life!' But, instead, I smiled and proceeded to ignore him."

"Nice going Sarina. He opens up to you and is rewarded with a blank stare and judgment. You're a peach."

"You're right, I suck as a girlfriend. Thanks." My sarcasm was palpable.
"Hey, you're taking this really seriously, aren't you honey?"

"Yeah, I am. I don't appreciate being attacked on the air."

I stood up, collected my things, and tightened my torn coat around me. "Hey, poignant message aside, you know I've got your back. I'm always here for you, no matter what." And with that, Eric softened.

I could feel myself starting to crack. Eric has a way of getting under my armor, but I wasn't ready to stop being mad.

"Close the show for me. I'm done. The doctor is out."

"No problem. Hey, remember we're still meeting at Muddy Waters later."

But, I was half way out the door and didn't reply.

The Lone Wolf

Lone

1. Having no one else around

2. Only or sole

3. Situated in an isolated position

Wolf

1.   any one of several predatory animals of North America and Eurasia that are related to the dog and hunt in packs, especially the gray wolf. Genus: Canis

Encarta® World English Dictionary © 1999 Microsoft Corporation. All rights reserved. Developed for Microsoft by Bloomsbury Publishing Plc.

I'm nothing but a lone wolf, misunderstood and labeled to be dangerous.

-Bela Lugosi

Imagine it. You've just made love to the most mysterious, amazing person ever. Although you've know each other for weeks (to let the tension build), you still know very few details about this incredible person. You have brought him or her home for the first time, had fantastic sex, and now you will cuddle up together in pre-matrimonial bliss and plan your future together. Okay, maybe not, but for sure it's time to open up and get to know each other better now. Maybe over breakfast after you wake in each others' arms?

"That was incredible. I knew we would connect like this," you say dreamily while covering your lover with kisses. "I have something special for us to share. Don't go away."

Because you are a great host, you pad on over to the kitchen and make some yummy, spiced, hot chocolate for the two of you. You are clad in your birthday suit and admire a reflection of yourself on the stove (Hey, it's your fantasy. If you want to look like a naked rock star, go for it.). You are smiling like the cat that swallowed the canary. You stir the cocoa and enjoy the warm aroma of chocolate and spice while you revisit the evening's festivities in your mind. You must admit you were great.

Then, you fill the mugs with the aromatic concoction, spoon on dollops of fresh whipped cream, pick up a mug in each hand, turn toward the kitchen door, and…

Almost like an apparition, your lover steps in the doorway. Suddenly, you are the only naked person in the room. You are holding a mug of spiced cocoa. Your lover is holding a set of car keys. What?

"Early day tomorrow. I really need to head out", your date says, and strides toward you.

"Umm, I made you some cocoa," is all you can think to say.

"You're very sweet. Another time, perhaps."

And with that, you are given a warm confusing kiss and left holding your cocoa, naked, and stunned into silence.

Now, if you are an adult, you know that the old "Early day tomorrow" ploy is just a polite excuse to get the hell out. It's right up there with, "It's not you, it's me." and "The dog ate my homework". Regardless, out the door they go.

Hate to say it, but once that door shuts, if this is a true Lone Wolf, your sweetheart is probably feeling like someone just took a tourniquet off his or her ribcage. Nothing but relief, baby.

Lone Wolves are people who are sincerely at peace alone. They eat, drink, and have sex just like everyone else. But, when the festivities are over, initially they may prefer their personal space to that of, say, yours. They also tend to need space and time for thinking and decision making.

Here's what you need to know. Any attempt to disturb this much needed space will result in repelling this Personality Type. Asking for something they don't have to offer will make them uncomfortable. Even the mere act of covering them with kisses after sex and jumping up to make them a cocoa could be construed as expecting too much, too soon. If you are a Lone Wolf, you will understand that last statement. If you're not, you are probably confused that such sweet acts of kindness could be viewed as a turn off.

Now, if one was to say, "Hey, I'm making myself a spiced cocoa. Want one?" That may not startle the Wolf. Why? You are doing something for yourself, and they are not obliged to participate to ensure your happiness. If they say no, no one gets hurt. And that is what keeps our Lone Wolves coming back. Once they see that you do not need them to be happy, they relax. Over time, they will come sniffing around to see what mysteries you conceal if they are fascinated or interested.

There is nothing wrong with these folks. As a matter of fact, they can be exquisite in their capacity to leave plenty of breathing room for a relationship to age naturally.

A little know fact about the Lone Wolf is that they tend to love quite ferociously if you just leave them alone long enough to build sincere fondness. They are not cold or unfeeling by any means. Quite the opposite. In their personal lives, Wolves tend to be internal and private, but also passionate and vulnerable people.

Lone Wolves should partner with other Lone Wolves if at all possible. They will, by nature, give each other space to breath and grow. They will understand when their partners choose to go for a walks alone to think things through. They will not pester each other out of a relationship. Lone Wolf couples tend to have artistic, creative, and successful lives together. This is due to their natural tendency toward cultivating and refining the object of their attention. Children of Lone Wolves are independent and self-assured.

As a Couple Personality Type, these guys are the cool cats. Well, maybe they're the dapper dogs.

Part 4

Muddy Waters 3pm

"The relationship guru doesn't need her boyfriend up her ass in this pivotal point in her career," I said. "What bugs me is how bad this is going to look. I mean, I have a meeting with GP tomorrow. I could be syndicated next month." Silence for a moment; then I continued. "I could also be homeless soon. How's that going to look? I'm going to be a laughing stock."

"My how you do go on, my little drama queen," Eric replied. "Why are you playing the victim card now? Brad's just being a nice guy. All he wants is to spend time with his woman. "Oh, catastrophe!"
I held my tongue. I wanted to hold his . . . and then rip it out. As I looked around our favorite little coffee shop, I saw trendy street kids sipping coffee and laughing. Piercings and dreds were everywhere - welcome to Minneapolis. I saw a twenty something couple doing a crossword together. Their dreds intertwined as they leaned in over the newspaper.

Under the table, I noticed their Birkenstocks gently touching. It was so simple; so easy. I got the feeling these kids had figured something out that I hadn't yet. Why wasn't Brad's love enough to keep me in love like these kids?

"Listen," Eric continued, "I like Brad a lot, but you gotta do what's best for you. Your public will be fine. Couple Chat will be fine. GP will be fine. It's all good. Just be ready for tomorrow. GP needs to meet the happy, successful woman they hear on the radio."

I snorted. "Oh. They don't want to syndicate the psycho who dumps perfectly great guys for no apparent reason?"

"No, doll. They don't."

"Look, I'm just worried that my relationship problems will screw everything up. You have to admit, it doesn't make me look good."

"Sweetie, I love you dearly, but sometimes you go a little overboard. This paranoid scenario you've whipped up isn't real. It's all in your head."

"Just 'cause you're paranoid doesn't mean they're not out to get you," I said trying not to smile.

"Funny, Sarina. Listen, the end of this story's already been written. It's only how you get there that you're affecting. It can be a smooth road or rocky road. It's up to us how we live into it. So, take a chill pill and relax."

And with that, Eric stood up, pulled me to my feet and gave me a big hug.

8pm that night

I rang the doorbell and waited. I rang again. Finally, Jacob, came to the door. He had coiffed hair and was wearing one of those tight look-at-my-big-guns shirts. That and the fact that he was blocking the door with his body instead of inviting me in told me he wasn't alone.

"Was I expecting you?" he asked, pretending not to notice my suitcases.

"Not really," I said. "Brad asked me to marry him." I just blurted it out. I thought it would be less painful that way. It wasn't.

"So you packed your bags and left?"

"Yes."

I've known Jacob for years. He is my producer and one of those friends who doesn't get too intimate. I needed that sometimes. Tonight, I needed a place to crash and he had an apartment.
Jacob put a consoling hand on my shoulder, and with that, I had to stop talking just to avoid sobbing. I wasn't feeling so high and mighty now. My reaction to Brad's proposal had been less than kind. What had started out as a romantic moment had quickly turned into another argument.

But, I was asking for space, and his answer was to ask me to marry him? What the hell?! How insensitive. As far as I was concerned, he deserved exactly what he got. I was right, dammit, and I knew it.

Jacob sighed heavily and stepped aside. I picked up my bags, but he took them from me.

"Sarina, this is Stephanie. Stephanie, this is Sarina." He had made the introductions without stopping as he walked my bags to the spare bedroom.

The tall blonde was sitting on the couch with a glass of red wine in her hand. She was young and gorgeous. She had applied full war paint and wore a sweater that was just low enough to be inappropriate for work, but perfect for a date.

Jacob was on a date and I had just crashed it. Oops. It was too late now. It didn't really bother me that much. Jacob has had a lot of dates.

"Hi, I'm sorry, what was your name again?" No reason to be rude to Barbie.

"Stephanie," Jacob shouted from the bedroom.

"I'm so sorry I'm bugging you guys," I said. "I'm an old friend of Jacob's. I'll just be in the spare room. You won't even know I'm here."

I followed Jacob into the room. He had already set my bags down when I'd shut the door behind me. He just stood there and stared at me. You know, that annoyed look you give a precious puppy after it tracks mud over your freshly mopped floor.

"You did tell me you would be here for me," I said, looking up at him with my best puppy-dog eyes.

"Yes. Yes I did."

"Surprise! Here I am. Slumber party at Jacob's! Wahoo!" I said all this trying to be fun and perky, but feeling like shit.

I thought he was going to kill me. There was a moment when the look in his eye told me it could have gone either way. Instead, he just smiled and said, "Make yourself at home." Then he turned around and let himself out, shutting the door quietly behind him, leaving me alone with my thoughts and jumbled emotions. It took about 45 seconds for me to burst into tears. It took another forty-five seconds for me to pull out my mobile and phone Sheila.

Sheila is a very cool friend of mine who always has the perfect advice when I run dry. She told me to put on some tight jeans, a pretty sweater, and some high-heeled boots and go the most expensive martini bar I could find - maybe two. She said she had a feeling about this one and that I should just do it. Sheila is a psychic. When she says I should do something, I usually listen.

Fifteen minutes later I strutted out of my new bedroom, past Jacob and Barbie having dinner, and out into the blustery Minneapolis night in search of an expensive martini and some answers.

By 9 pm I was snugly at Blue, the bar at the Grand Hotel. It wasn't really my thing, but it was close to Jacob's and served the finest liquor available.

"Tequila martini, please. Lemon; not a twist, but actually squeeze fresh lemon juice in, please; shaken in a cold glass."

"Coming right up, ma'am." Again with the 'ma'am.

I put my head in my hands, closed my eyes, and took a deep breath. The events of the last few hours rolled in my mind like a movie. Brad's apartment filled with flowers. A candle lit dinner for two. And there I was, the bull in the china shop, showing zero appreciation. Leave it to me to ruin a romantic moment. Why couldn't I just appreciate this wonderful, sensitive man? I mean, I loved him, didn't I? Why did I always feel like he wanted something I couldn't give? Why couldn't I just relax and accept this relationship? What was wrong with me?

The martini was delicious. As I sipped my drink from a fine crystal glass and let the day roll off my back, I felt someone staring at me. When I glanced at the end of the bar, I swear I saw the same guy I ran into earlier in the coffee shop. He was looking at me with curiosity. I looked away, but he got up and walked over.

"Café miel. Soy, decaf." The handsome stranger said in my ear. The electricity between us was almost palpable. I could feel his breath against my ear. I never felt like this around Brad. Normally, stunts like this made my skin crawl. I have a pretty strong sense of personal space, and most people aren't allowed to cross it. However, this time it didn't creep me out. Weird.

"Don't bother with a to-go cup. I prefer to wear mine," I said without looking up. My voice dropped in register as the sexy came out. God, I'm suave. He laughed under his breath, and in that instant I miraculously remembered his name. "Are you stalking me, Gary Parker? That's kind of creepy, you know."

Again he laughed. "It looks like that, I'm sure. But really, I'm just here for a meeting tomorrow."
"You were in the neighborhood and thought you'd drop in? You need to work on your pickup lines, Mr. Parker. They're outdated."

"Very funny. Actually I'm staying in the neighborhood."

"You're staying here?" I asked.

"Yes. Are you?"

"No. I'm staying at a different place up the street."

"You never did tell me your name," Gary said inquisitively.

I looked him in the eye for the first time. Electricity. Oh, God no. Not now. "Ss-ss-sss," I stammered.

"I'm sorry?" he said.

"Ss-Sarah. Sarah Hart." It was out of my mouth before I could stop myself. It would be the name Gary Parker, stud extraordinaire, would know me by.

It occurred to me as he eyed me for a moment, that this may have been what Sheila thought I would find. But was this really what I wanted to be doing just hours after I walked out on the most wonderful man I've ever dated?

I looked at him again. This time I really took him in. He wore his dark, thick hair sort of disheveled, just long enough to cover his ears and neck. His brown eyes were that golden color I've seen on Israeli men, and his nose was small and straight. What I could not take my eyes off were his lips. They were full and perfectly shaped. I found myself staring, not speaking.

"Nice to meet you, Sarah. Mind if I sit down?" he asked, pointing to the empty stool beside me.

"I'm just finishing my drink, but you're welcome to sit for a few minutes." I said.

Four hours later, three tequila martinis for me and three for Gary, we were laughing our heads off as he walked me to the front door to catch a taxi back to Jacob's.

Maybe it was the tequila, maybe it was the stress of leaving Brad, and maybe it was the fact that Gary was a beautiful stranger I'd never see again. Or maybe it was that gnawing feeling that I knew Gary much better than I should have in the short time we'd spent together. Whatever the reason, I let him kiss me goodnight. It was one of those kisses that starts sweet and slow, then turns into the kind of thing that leads to something more.

"Stay," Gary whispered, and it sent shivers down my spine.
"Thanks, but no," I said. Not bad for a lady whose knees were shaking.
Then he said something that changed everything. "To me . . . you are perfect."

Perfect. Wow. Something about that word melted the last bit of fight I had inside. I looked at this man and now he looked totally different. He looked pure and open. I could feel his yearning, and it wasn't creepy. It was beautiful.

Maybe it was just a huge rush of Oxytocin, but in an instant, he looked different to me. I noticed everything. I saw how well-coiffed he was. I hadn't really noticed before, but his teeth were perfect and his skin was amazing, too. He had the most beautiful gold and black diamond cufflinks adorning his perfectly fitted, perfectly pressed, un-tucked dress shirt. His shoes were comfortable and understated, but obviously expensive (He had big shoes, too. You know what they say about men with big feet.). Upon closer inspection, I got the distinct impression that this man looked casual, but was actually quite artful with his presentation. There are people in this world who see art in every day objects. Like Ayn Rand describing art deco architecture, some people just get it. This man was more than nice teeth and pretty cufflinks; he had grace and sublime style. How could I have missed that until just this moment?

"No promises, Gary." I said.

With that Gary Parker grabbed my hand, dismissed the taxi, and led me back inside the Grand Hotel.

Sybil Couples

The snow goose needs not bathe to make itself white. Neither need you do anything but be yourself.

-Laozi

For those who never read the book Sybil, allow me to explain. There was a woman who was terribly abused by her mother as she was growing up. In order to cope with the pain and betrayal, the main character's brain created multiple personalities to handle various situations. These personalities came through this woman as distinct people, with distinct and separate abilities and agendas. The story walks its reader through sessions with a psychiatrist who attempts to help by introducing her personalities to each other. The psychiatrist was ultimately successful and the patient's many personalities ultimately became one, whole being.

The patient's name was Sybil.

Sybil Couples are the kind of people one may watch at a public function and think, "Gee, I'd love to have a partner like that." She always speaks so highly of him, and he is never caught glancing at another woman. They are kind to each other. They support each other. I mean, it's just like those couples you see on television.

Again, it's just like those couples you see on television. It's all staged and it's all fake.

Why would I mention these couples when it seems the only people who would project a controlled public image are people in either entertainment or politics? It is because I see this crazy repression of the truth everywhere. Corporate America is notorious for it. Family gatherings are riddled with it. But the biggest reason normal people keep up a façade is because they are too afraid to move forward with a separation and don't want to talk about it.

The image of partnership is a part of the illusion the Sybil Couple feels they need to project for or to their community. The fact that they can't stand each other does not matter to them as long as the people around them think they're just great.

Oddly enough, I see this Couple Personality Type more than any other. I chose to write about it here, with very little humor, because I would like to say once and for all, "Wow. That sucks."

The amount of energy it takes to remain in a dead relationship is indeterminate. What we do know is that living a lie eventually sucks the life out of both partners. We are shocked when we find that guy who never gets caught looking at other woman has a lover on the side. We are shocked to find that woman who always speaks highly of her partner actually insists on sleeping in separate beds.

But golly, they just look so great together.

Probably the top two excuses for couples to stay together for years after the relationship has faded are children and money. I have addressed the issue of setting examples for kids in another part of this book, so I won't reiterate too much. I will suffice to say this, "It doesn't work. It never did. It never will."

As for the money issue - get a job or a lawyer. You'll be much happier.

If you are a Sybil Couple, you know who you are. My heart goes out to you and my prayer is that you take better care of yourselves and start leading lives with nothing to hide. The air out here is calm, come take a deep breath.

Part 5

Most people wake up from a night of drinking looking like hell. I am not one of those people. I think it's because alcohol is a diuretic and I look skinny from being so dehydrated. Maybe it's because I drink so infrequently that blowing off a little steam is like therapy. Regardless, the previous night I'd blown off a lot of steam and in the morning I had that tousled-but-well-rested look when I crept into Gary Parker's the hotel bathroom.

"What were you thinking?" I said aloud to my own face in the mirror. I sat down on the tile floor and started to cry. I would bet my bank account Brad had never cheated on me. I know this wasn't technically cheating because we had separated, but it sure felt like it.

How did I get myself into this? I'm supposed to be an expert on dating and intimacy. Where was that woman now? What would she do? What would Sarina Stone, Relationship Expert, do in a situation like this? Truth be told, she wouldn't be in this mess. Apparently that Sarina's a lot smarter than this one.

After a while, I pulled myself together, un-wrapped a toothbrush on the counter, and brushed my teeth. It felt good to do something normal. Plus, I had that lovely taste in my mouth like something crawled in there and died last night, so this was sort of a necessity.

I dared not wash my face because that would remove all my make-up and I wouldn't want to completely ruin the illusion for Gary. I took a military shower (sponge bath washing the pits and privates), then wrapped myself in a large towel and walked out of the bathroom. Mr. Parker was wide awake and talking on the phone.

"Yeah. I want to reschedule for 12pm. Trust me, it'll be fine." he said and hung up.

The illustrious Gary Parker locked fabulous sprawled out on the huge four-poster bed in the morning sun. He never took his eyes off of me as he was talking. He continued to watch me as he hung up and motioned for me to come back to bed.

I stood there for a moment struggling with my conflicting emotions. Wasn't that just me weeping on the bathroom floor? Am I not the Sarina Stone that railed against people with Low Integrity Syndrome? And yet, here I was, about to do it all again. I felt a pang of guilt as the towel dropped away. But, it was just like the first time we met. Electric. I completely lost my inhibitions, and went to him.

I was doomed.

At 9:30am, we were sipping coffee and munching on croissants. Gary read the paper and I did the crossword. I looked at my watch and said, "I have a meeting at 11am. I better get going."

The moment I said that, my phone rang. It was Jacob.

"You okay?"

"Yeah. I'm on my way actually."

Jacob continued to speak as I got up and checked the room for any objects I may have left behind. Some jewelry and my purse were on the nightstand next to my panties. Nice.

"I'm going to grab a cup of java," he continued.

"Hey. I'm a mile away. Wait for me and we'll go together," I said and hung up. "Gary, I have to go. I need to prep for that meeting."

"That's right," he said. "Your boss is being reviewed today."

I told Gary that I was a personal assistant to a "celebrity." I described her as a terrific boss and chose to keep her name out of it. A lie? Oh, yeah. I just wanted to be a normal person having a normal date. I had no idea I would end up spending the night with him. Now, he wanted my phone number. My business card had my real name on it. So, I wrote down a fake phone number to match my fake name. I scooped up my jewelry and underwear off the nightstand, threw them into my bag and kissed Gary Parker one last time. I was panty-less and a little paranoid, but still had control of my faculties enough to be cool and collected.

Last night would be our little secret. At least I didn't have to see him again. I intended to give him a quick peck goodbye and it turned in to a five-minute make out session. I really had to get out of there!
I flagged a taxi and was back at Jacob's place in a few minutes.

"Well. Look what the cat dragged in."

Funny guy, that Jacob.

"Did you go back to your place last night, because you didn't come home to mine."

"It was an interesting evening. Can we get in to it later? I need a shower, but I can be ready in thirty minutes," I said. "You can give me shit after the meeting."

The water felt great. I so needed to wash the past 24 hours off my skin. Don't get me wrong, Prince Charming was wonderful, handsome, smart, and if memory serves, rich. I hate to kiss and tell, but he was epic in the bedroom. I don't know precisely how to explain it, but with Gary, I could feel that he was with me. Sometimes people have sex just for the pleasure of it, but sometimes lovers connect with each other because they each want to be close to that specific individual. Gary was bold enough to connect with me in an open loving way, and I lost myself in his embrace almost immediately. Time stood still in our bed.

But Gary wasn't enough to take Brad off my mind. In the light of day, I just felt like hell. I felt like I cheated. In a way, I think I did. As I stood in the shower, I took a good look at my behavior with Brad and started hating myself. All he wanted was someone to walk the world with. Why did his need for intimacy spark such a defensive reaction in me? It wasn't like he was creepy or over the top. As a matter of fact, Brad was probably the kindest, most self-secure man I'd ever dated. It was his strength and independence that inspired me to move in with him. He was the only man I'd been intimate with who didn't find my career intimidating. He had his own thing going as a lawyer, and he certainly understood how time consuming a career could be. Somehow, I had started to view the moments he craved with me as a burden. Why couldn't I just be madly in love with this guy?

Thirty minutes later, I was clean, polished, and ready to face the day. At least I looked like I was. Jacob and I walked to another favorite coffee house, the Sawatdee Cup. They have one in Chiang Mai, and my adventures with my old pal Mordant had quickly embedded this as "home" in my mind. We chatted about where we were headed with the show. Very soon we would be sitting across from a man who had the power to make me a national radio star. GP Enterprises owned radio and television stations across the United States and into Canada. If they wanted Couple Chat on their radio stations, it would just be a matter of time before affiliates started taking notice. Billboards and advertisements would be part of the deal. Eventually, my advice column, Quantum Love, would also become syndicated. This is how you build celebrity in my arena. This meeting had potential for being a serious turning point for both of us, as I intended to request Jacob's continued participation behind the scenes.
"Oh, I forgot to tell you," Jacob said. "We have extra time. GP pushed the meeting back an hour."

"I'll check my calendar and see if I can squeeze it in."

Jacob's eyes sparkled "So . . . you gonna give me details about last night?"

"Why should I? You never kiss and tell." As soon as I said it, I wanted to take it back.

"Aha! So you met someone! I knew it."
Yeah. He was a regular Sherlock Holmes.

Fighter Couples

1.   A fighter is somebody who is very determined and struggles hard
      to achieve or resist something
2.   A fighter is somebody who takes part in boxing matches

Encarta® World English Dictionary © 1999 Microsoft Corporation. All
rights reserved. Developed for Microsoft by Bloomsbury Publishing Plc.

*"A wise man fights to win, but he is twice a fool who has no plan
for possible defeat."*

-Louis L'Amour

These guys are a riot! I don't mean that in the hilariously zany
way, I mean they fight all the time.
Fighters are those crazy couples that simply cannot hold back their
animosity toward their partners, even in public. They will debate the
smallest issues with ferocity pretty much anywhere or any time. They
tend not to care for the delicate sensibilities of those around them when
they get on a roll. Most of us know at least one couple like this and they
can be spotted, or rather heard, a mile away.

My favorite, and yes, I'm being sarcastic, is when they try to
pull others into the debate. Oh yeah, we get to play! Even the ludicrous
suggestion that they continue this argument at home could be an invitation
to join the fun, so be careful.
I remember a dinner in Mexico, years ago, with about one half dozen
friends. Two at the table were married, the rest just single folks. I don't
remember what started it, but before hors d'oeuvres were served, the
married couple was arguing intensely. She was shouting. He was not too
quiet either. The rest of us got up, one by one, and went to the bar. It was
many minutes before they even noticed we were gone.

Obnoxious? Yes. Headed for failure? Here's what's really odd
about Fighter Couples – they frequently stay together forever. I think it
may be because they know exactly where they stand with each other. Or

maybe they stay together because they finally found someone who loves to argue as much as they do. Maybe being right and proving it is fun for them. Regardless, they are a real Couples Personality Type. One cannot label these people right or wrong, just monotonous at times.

I suppose a Fighter partnered with a more passive personality would just become a Dreaded Control Freak? Perhaps. But I am a purist and suggest Fighters partner with fighters. You will find each other stimulating. The rest of us will bring earplugs.

Part 6

At noon, we were seated in a trendy Minneapolis restaurant, the
Loring Pasta Bar, waiting for the representative from GP Enterprises.
We had no idea what their rep or reps looked like, so we left our names
at the door. I was nervous. Jacob never shows unease, thank God.
I excused myself to go freshen up and do a little breathing. I stood in
front of the mirror and took a couple of deep breaths to calm myself.
"This is it," I said aloud. I held out my hand to see how steady it was.
Only shook a little bit – points for me. I stole a few more minutes
by re-applying my lipstick. Hell, I even checked my stockings for
snags. With nothing left to waste time, and no time left to waste, I
turned around, walked through the door, and left the safety of the little
bathroom. All things considered, I felt pretty good.

I walked with a confident stride and a big smile through the dining
room. I had my game face on. I saw that Jacob was sitting with
someone already. It was time to play.

As I approached the table, I could see the back of the other man's head.
Neat. They sent us a guy, so I adjusted my blouse and straightened
up even more. As I got closer, I noticed something oddly familiar. I
knew the curl of his hair; I knew the shape of his shoulders.

I froze in my tracks. Oh, come on! Though I'd only known him for
twenty-four hours, I knew this man - intimately. Gary Parker was
sitting at the table with Jacob.
There was no way that my Gary Parker was the representative of GP
Enterprises. All the synapses in my brain began to fire. One right
after another, everything began to fall into place. Gary Parker. GP
Enterprises. Gary Parker Enterprises.

Oh Shit. No fricking way.

I was kidding when I said this before, but it's true. I was doomed and I'd doomed us all.

I will attempt to relay the next series of incidences as accurately as I can. Just as I was desperately trying to get Jacob's attention, Jacob's attention fell to Gary. So there I was, using sign language, and I don't know sign language, on a guy who wasn't even looking. Since I wasn't able to quickly and accurately relay that I needed to go now, I just spun around to exit before Gary saw me.

As I turned to the door, timed slowed; it was just like the movies. In my haste to leave, I managed to slam into a waiter who was hidden behind me. This caused him to lose his center of gravity and perform what may be the most interesting balancing act with a tray of full coffee cups I've seen to date. I don't know how, but the two of us managed not to fall onto one of the full tables. However, the coffee flew everywhere, and the chaos was substantial.

What were the odds? Two ruined blouses in one week. Was the Universe trying to tell me something? Was coffee evil? Were blouses evil? Had I missed my calling as a stunt-woman?

All eyes were on us. The waiter straightened up and shook it off. I straightened up and shook it off. What I couldn't shake off was the fact that Gary Parker was looking right at me.

Of course, Gary stood up when I approached the table. Whereas five minutes ago I was clean, polished and confident, the rustic mirrors around us now reflected disheveled hair and a coffee stained blouse. Gary was fabulous as he extended his hand to fake saying hello to me for the first time. I wanted to die, but put a smile on my face and took a deep breath to introduce myself. Gary beat me to the punch.

He smiled warmly as he said, "You must be Sarah –"

"Sarina," I quickly interjected, "Sarina Stone. Nice to meet you." Gary smirked "Do I know you?" he asked. "Haven't we bumped in to each other before? "That shirt. It's oddly familiar."

Apparently, I was bumping into a lot of people these days. I really didn't know what to do. Here I was again, with egg on my face and coffee stains on my blouse.

Jacob chimed in, "Am I missing something?"

"Sarina and I ran into each other yesterday," Gary said as he moved behind me and pulled out my chair. He looked like the cat that swallowed the canary. I wanted to throttle him. "Actually, she ran in to me," he said with a sly grin and positioned himself to look me dead in the eye now.

"What?" asked Jacob.

"Yeah, we just happened to be at the same coffee shop yesterday morning," Gary said. "What are the chances? Isn't that the same shirt you were wearing yesterday?"

He had smiled as he said it, but the comment sent a cold chill down my spine. "W-What?" I stammered.

"You know; the one with the coffee stains."

Gary was all smiles as he said this. I sat there laughing nervously. Jacob was looking back and forth between us like he was watching a tennis match.

"Actually it's a different blouse," I came back, trying to be nonchalant, "but I think it's the same flavor of coffee. I hope it's decaf."

"If the two of you don't mind," Jacob said, "I'd like to give Mr. Parker our press kit and get the ball rolling."

"Actually, you can keep the press kit," Gary said.

This was it. This was the part where he told us that his media conglomerate was not interested in backing slutty on-air personalities. I held my breath as I watched him pull something from his briefcase and lower the boom.

"My company has everything it needs from you." As he said this, he threw out another copy of our press kit onto the table. And there it was: my face, on the cover and my name as clear as day. He had known all along exactly who I was. I wanted to kill him.

The next few minutes were a blur of conversation about the show and what GP Enterprises wanted to do about it. Jacob and Gary did all of the talking. I was too busy trying not to do anything further to embarrass myself.

Eventually, Jacob excused himself and went to the bathroom. I took that moment to come back to my senses and go on the offensive.

"You lied to me!" I said with an air of indignity.

"Me? I lied?" he said feigning shock and disbelief.

"Well, I'm glad you admit it," I said. "I can't believe that you knew exactly who I was the whole time we were together."

"Of course I did," Gary said. "I don't move forward on a project without doing the proper research."

"Is that what I was to you - research?"
"Well, yes and no. I wasn't expecting to get to know you so–"

"Deeply?!" I interrupted.

"Actually, I was going to say intimately, but thanks for the compliment."
"Whatever. Don't get cute with me—I'm still mad at you. And another thing, how did you know I would even be at the coffee shop,

Mr. Stalker?"

"I didn't."

"Oh yeah, well what about the martini bar?" I asked accusingly. "Pure coincidence, I swear. You know that I'm staying at the hotel. I had no idea that you would show up that night. When you did, I decided it was time to introduce myself. This was not premeditated, Sarah, I mean, Sarina." With that he smiled that handsome smile of his, and I began to melt.

I have to admit, the series of events was uncanny, but not out of the realm of possibility, especially considering my background in Quantum Manifestation. As angry as I wanted to be, I felt a connection with this man. I didn't know if he was the messenger or the message, but he was something. It was too soon to say why we'd been drawn together, but there was that old familiar crackle in the air. Something was going on; I just wasn't sure what yet.

Here's a clue, if you didn't glean this from the first book, synchronicities are nature's way of telling you to pay attention. I can't tell you the whats or whys, but watch for these synchronicities because they are leading you to the place you probably need to see for your own personal growth. Living in the mystery and trusting the process is the mark of a wise and connected person.

I may not have been behaving like a wise person but I knew my metaphysical signs, and Gary Parker was "a thing" whether I liked it or not.

"Well, it doesn't appear as if I've ruined things for Jacob and I and GP Enterprises," I said. "That's a relief. So, where do we go from here?"

"If by we you mean you and your cohort, we let the lawyers handle that. But, if by we you mean you and I . . . I think you're an amazing woman, and I'm not afraid to pursue what feels right. I need to see you again, Sarina. Tonight, if possible."

"What?" I said with all the grace of a deer in the headlights.

"What'd I miss?" Score a point for Jacob and his impeccable timing.

"I was just telling your business partner, before Quantum Dating Club and GP get into bed together, I need to get to know you better. I don't mean to thrust myself upon you but I need to get to know you on a more intimate level. With your permission, I'm going to be inserting myself into your lives for a while."

Did he just say that?

"Sounds good to me," Jacob said.

What?!

"Let us know what you need. We're wide open." Jacob continued. Ok, where was the hidden camera? Was Allen Funt hiding somewhere?

All I could think was, my life is hell.

Bliss Eater Couples

Bliss (n)
1.   Perfect untroubled happiness
2.   A state of spiritual joy

Eater (n)
A person who or animal that eats a particular food or eats in a particular way (often used in combination)

"Your task is not to seek for love, but merely to seek and find all the barriers within yourself that you have built against it."

-Rumi

Oxytocin (n)
A hormone released by the pituitary gland that stimulates contractions of the womb during childbirth and triggers the secretion of milk from the breast during nursing.

Oh, please. That is such a half hearted explanation of the effects of Oxytocin. I mean, yes, this hormone does all that. But it also makes that mom look at her new born and be 100% convinced that this is the most incredible, intelligent child on the planet. Oxytocin literally has the ability to change the way some people feel about others when their cellular receptors are flooded with and absorbing it. Oxytocin is a powerful hormone and has been the cause of a lot of romantic confusion.
Let's move on. Bliss Eater Couples are fantastic. They are the wacky couples who you find making out in the restaurant. You want to say, "Hey! Get a room." And then,"How wonderful to be so in love."

Bliss Eaters are people who value romance and passion above intellect. They find reasons to be in love based on the signs from their body and heart. They are the romantics.

Bliss eater Couples come in a few categories.

We have our Fledglings. These are the new lovers who simply cannot get enough of each other. They are sincerely in love. Not much more to say here, except "congratulations."

We have our Serial Bliss Eaters. Remember the Fantasy Addict from Why Real Women Drink Straight Tequila? The Serial Bliss Eaters are what you get when you put two of these people together. If you have not read the book, you should. Bottom line – a Serial Bliss Eater jumps in while the sexy romantic feelings are high and leaves when it's over. Although temporary, these couples exist. If there is even a chance you are one of those couples, I highly recommend not making any long-term commitments.

Last, and my favorite (no sarcasm), are the Old Timers. These people have taken years to get to know each other, and are more in love and attracted to their partners than ever.

We love our Bliss Eaters, regardless of their longevity, because they remind us of the warmth and, well, bliss of being in love.

We cringe when they break commitments and show up late because they were "doing it" again. Yes, it can be a bit much if their public displays of affection are grotesque or inappropriate. But this is what they do. Look away if you must, but sneak a peak to remind yourselves that wild abandon is still alive and well.

Part 7

"I think that went swimmingly well," beamed Jacob, finishing his Thai iced coffee.

"You have got to be kidding me. That was probably the single most nerve-wracking experience of my life. Do you know who that guy was, Jacob?" I damn near shouted.

"Yeah, he's Gary Parker, CEO of GP Enterprises. He's the guy who's going to make us rich and you famous. If I was a drinker, I'd have one of those Tequila Martinis in a fine crystal glass right about now. But, I'll settle for this adrenal- rockin' coffee instead. Wahoo, Tao sister, we're gonna be famous!"

Jacob tried to toast with me by raising his glass. I just sat there. "What the heck is wrong with you?" Jacob asked with an air of irritability. "We finally get the big break we've been waiting for and all you can do is sulk. You barely participated in the conversation today. God! The only time I see you get this quiet is when we run into one of your exes..."

The light went off on top of Jacob's head. First he looked shocked, like he just remembered he left the iron on. Then he looked puzzled and sort of tilted his head and looked at me funny. I just sat there.

Eventually, his eyes narrowed, "You never did tell me where you were last night. I think you better tell me now."

"Well," I said quietly, "I sort of had one of those crazy, didn't see it coming, way out of left field experiences last night." I struggled for words that may have redeemed my actions. "Look, there are no lies here. Brad let me go. He probably slept with someone, too," I said not believing a word of it. "Besides, Sheila sent me out on a mission and I think I stumbled in to it. It's really quite healthy and empowering."

"Bullcrap, cut to the chase. Who were you with last night, Stone?"

"Would you believe I just happened to run in to Mr. GP Enterprises at the Grand Hotel last night? I mean, what are the chances. It was like kismet."
This last line was said with a toothy smile which begged not be punched. And then Jacob did something I never would have seen coming. He stood up, pulled out a twenty dollar bill, threw it on the table, and put on his coat.

"Look, I used an alias. And how the heck was I supposed to know that Gary Parker stood for GP? He wasn't exactly forthcoming and I wasn't so open with the personal info either. It was supposed to be anonymous," I explained. "He deceived me! If you're gonna be mad, be mad at him. He knew who I was the whole time and went along with it."

I stood up and tried to approach Jacob. "Hey sweetie," I gently said. "Don't! Just don't." he said with tight lips. "You should have told me."

"But I didn't…"

Jacob left me standing alone. Without saying a word, he just split. It seemed like a big spotlight was on moi. I felt like everyone knew my friend just walked out on me, my boyfriend kicked me out, and I had just slept with my boss. I was wearing an invisible scarlet letter, and the people in that room could see it.

I didn't stay long. I paid and left. When I got to my car, there was a parking ticket on the windshield, of course.

I looked up at the sky and shouted for all to hear "Why me?"

And where was I supposed to go? Jacob was furious with me and Brad didn't want me in his house either. Oh, I guess I could go to the Grand Hotel and sell my soul to dickweed Parker, I mean Gary, and have a place to sleep. Oh, what a tangled web we weave when at first we practice to deceive. God, I hated when my mom used to say that to me. I hated it even worse now that I understood what it meant.

You could hear my resignation as I sighed aloud. I didn't want to go, but I knew exactly where I needed to be at a time like this. Though I was loath to admit it, there was only one place where I felt safe.

"Hi, mom."

My mother stood looking at me through the screen door. Her face was expressionless, a mask of noncommittal emotion. I'd seen it before —usually in the mirror. Maybe coming here was a mistake.

"Oh," she finally said, "is this a salesperson knocking on my door, or do I have a daughter now?" Mom can be the epitome of a Jewish mother when she feels like it. Look it up in the dictionary, and you'll see her picture there. She is an amazing cook, keeps her finger on the pulse of all of her kids, and is quick to dispense advice when she thinks you need it.

"Mom, please let me in. I've got no place else to go."

"Oh, my baby," she said, flinging the screen door open. She gave me a huge hug and that's when my emotional damn burst. She ushered me inside as the tears streamed down my face. In that moment, I could feel everything. All the anger, fear, worry, and anxiety came flooding into my consciousness in a huge wave. My heart ached. I could hardly stand it. And, all it took was a hug from my mommy. Oh yeah, I'm an adult.

"What happened, honey?" Mom sat me down on the couch in the living room. She fired concerned questions at me while she fixed a couple cups of tea. She didn't have to ask how I took it. She was my mom. She just knew.

"Everything's a mess, mom," I began. "Gary and I broke up."

"Gary? Who's Gary?"

Did I say Gary? Shit.

"Did I say Gary? I meant Brad."

"Honey, who's Gary?"

Yup, that's my mom. Nothing ever got past her. Dammit. It's no fun growing up with a psychic, especially when it came to being an unruly adolescent. Somehow, I still felt like a teenager around her sometimes.

"Gary's not important right now, Mom. Brad and I are in a rough patch. I moved out and I'm staying with Jacob, but now he and I are fighting, too. God! Everybody hates me!"

And with that, I cried even harder. I cried until I seemed to disappear and all that was left was sadness and guilt.

"Jacob's like your brother. It's natural."

I nodded my head.

"I don't know what to do this time. It's like I'm losing control of everything."

"That's because you try to hold on so tightly." She held up a hand before I could interrupt. "I know, I know. We create our own reality. You don't need to tell me; I taught it to you."

She was right. She was a life coach from way back.

"But, Mom, I'm trying so hard to be a decent human being, why is this happening to me?" Wow. A little cheese with that whine?

"Sarina, you can't control everything. Try to relax and go with the flow, honey."

"Do you think that this is just life being mysterious and strange; a bump in the road? It's not really me?" At last, a ray of hope.

"Oh no, dear. It's definitely you." A ray of hope eclipsed by mother's moon of sober reality.

Why did I bother to come here? If I wanted someone to dump on me, I could always call Jacob or Brad. Gary still liked me, but I'd be ruining that soon enough I'm sure. I grabbed my keys and stood up to go.

"Thanks for the pep talk, Mom. It's nice to see you haven't lost your bedside manner."

"Honey, you're not my client, you're my daughter. And you're just as good a life coach as I am—you know all this stuff already. You just can't see it because it's you this time."

"Isn't a life coach supposed to have her shit together? I mean, I have a relationship radio show, for chrissake!"

"You already have all your answers. You're just not ready to look at them yet. And, as far as life coaches and relationship gurus being perfect, you know better than that. We're just people."

"But, aren't we supposed to be more enlightened than the masses? That's why we teach."

"Enlightened doesn't mean perfect, dear. Just because we hear the answers doesn't mean we always listen. We're human, just like everybody else. It keeps things interesting. Remember, it's nothing serious—it's just your life." She started laughing hysterically and damned near fell over herself as she walked back to the kitchen.

It was just like Mom or Master Chia to say something like that. "Thanks, Mom," I shouted at the kitchen. "you've been almost no help at all." I said under my breath.

"I heard that." She chirped.

I suddenly got restless and stood up. Without so much as a 'good bye', I let myself out, leaving hot tea and a cool mother behind me. But, being my mom, she had to get in one last zinger. I heard the screen door open.

She shouted, "Pain is inherent, suffering is optional my dear." Of course, I slammed my car door in response. Ugh!

I'd barely made it in to the corner when my mobile rang. It was Brad. I just stared at it as the tears ran down my cheeks. I could not answer. I needed some time to myself. The beep rang through, telling me I had a voicemail, but I'd reached a full-on cry by that time and did not check it. Instead, I turned the corner and started driving to nowhere in particular.
45 minutes of driving had taken me to the old Mary Tyler Moore house in Minneapolis. My phone must have rung 3 or 4 times and I didn't answer. I was not in the mood.

Mary's house is a real house. It's the one they used in the TV show. Mary was one of my childhood heroes. I know it's silly, but connecting with her always reminded me that there is a bright side to everything.

After that, I drove a block to Lake of The Isles and tried to meditate for the first time in days. Unfortunately, the phone rang again and I never quite made it to that realm of undiluted potential.

"Did you hear?" It was Jacob.

"Hear what?"

"It's Brad. He's been in an accident. It's bad Sarina."

"That's impossible, he just called me," I said.

"I don't know what to tell you, all I know is that I just got a call from Abbott Hospital, looking for you. Both of our numbers are in Brad's ICE."

"What the hell is an ICE?"

"It's an emergency number programmed into a mobile phone under the name ICE. Paramedics know to look for this In Case of Emergency," Jacob said in a panic.

"Oh, my God. Brad tried to get me to do this months ago."

"Well, maybe you should. But right now, you need to get to the hospital."

I felt faint. "I know I don't deserve it, but would you meet me there?"

"I'm pulling up now, honey. I also called Eric and Sheila. See you when you get here."

Jacob hung up and I ran back to my car, fumbling for the keys. I started listening to my voice mails as soon as my phone connected to my hands-free device. The first voice to come over the stereo speakers was Brad's.

"Hi baby. I just wanted to tell you that the house hasn't been the same without you. I hate it when we fight—"

That's as far as his message went.

I drove on in horror as the sound of Brad's accident played in surround sound over my stereo speakers. My chest tightened as the crush of metal on metal cut through my body. I flinched involuntarily and swerved, narrowly missing another vehicle, as the sound of breaking glass came pouring out of my speakers. But it was Brad's screams of pain and surprise that stole the breath from me. I felt like I'd been kicked in the chest. I listened helplessly, my tears blinding me as I rushed to the hospital, and I screamed along with him in frustration.

It seemed to go on forever, before we were abruptly cut off. His phone went dead.

Next message, 30 minutes later, was Sheila. Jacob must have called her first.

"Honey, I'm sure you're on your way to the hospital. I'll meet you there. Don't worry, sweetie, we're visualizing a safe recovery already... "

Next was Eric "Hey, are you ok? I'm heading for the hospital in case you need me for anything. I'm so sorry, Sarina."

By now I was weaving through traffic when the next message came in. It was Abbott hospital.

"This is Abbott Northwest Hospital. We're trying to reach Sarina Stone. There's an accident victim here who's given your name as an Emergency Contact."

The hospital administrator droned on, giving their contact information, but the sound of my heart pounding out of my chest drowned it out. I hit the red button, cutting her off. I knew where I was going; I was only 15 minutes away.

I was stopped at a light when a wave of nausea swept over me. My stomach did flip flops, and I was on the verge of losing my lunch. Great, this was all I needed.

Mercifully, the nausea began to recede. Unmercifully, it was replaced by a crashing headache. It was a very particular kind of pain, and I knew it well.

"No! Not now!" I shouted aloud. Now was not the time to get one of my infamous visions.

My family is cursed with foresight. Actually, it's just the women in my family line. Some would call this a blessing—receiving cryptic messages about future possibilities—but believe me, it can be a curse. Just ask Joan of Arc.

I concentrated with everything I had and stuffed this vision back inside. I could feel it recede like an ocean tide, not really disappearing, just laying in wait for another opportunity. Whatever that is that watches over us all had decided that a "vision" while driving was a bad idea. Apparently, there were enough car crashes today.

So hang on Brad. Your girl is on her way.

You know how when you spend the night drinking large quantities of poor quality tequila you have that pivotal moment, usually viewing your own vomit in a place where other people crap, where you swear you will NEVER do this again. Interestingly enough, many people actually follow through on that because just the smell of cheap tequila will make them ill for years afterward. They also learn something about themselves. They have an epiphany. Self-abusive, gut rotting, cheap tequila is bad. They realize that drunken, obnoxious behavior is creepy and makes them feel like idiots.

The lucky come back to tequila later, but it will most certainly be a fine blend and will be used with mindfulness and in moderation. You know, like an adult. I found tequila and never looked back.
Then there are those poor saps who never get past the painful memory, and never experience the smooth sensations truly fine liquor brings to the table when enjoyed responsibly.

This was my epiphany when I heard that Brad was hurt. I had tequila and I treated him like he was Ripple. I refused to accept that he wouldn't hurt me, so I kept him away. Sure, I took a sip once in a while, but I never really appreciated and trusted him. All he wanted was intimacy, and I held it back.

Now, I may never have a chance to make things right. I may never wake up and literally smell the coffee, because that was Brad's job, and now Brad might be gone.

Baby Maker Couples

Baby (n)
1.   A very young child who is not yet able to walk or talk
2.   A child that is still in the womb
3.   Somebody who behaves childishly or is overly dependent on others

Maker (n)
1.   Somebody who creates something or is the source or cause of it
       (often used in combination)
2.   A person or organization that produces goods (often used in
       combination)
3.   Somebody who signs a promissory note

Encarta® World English Dictionary © 1999 Microsoft Corporation. All
rights reserved. Developed for Microsoft by Bloomsbury Publishing Plc.

*Children keep us in check. Their laughter prevents our hearts
from hardening. Their dreams ensure we never lose our drive to
make ours a better world. They are the greatest disciplinarians
known to mankind.*
- Queen Rania of Jordan, Hello Magazine

These couples fascinate me. Baby Maker Couples are people who
get pregnant right away. This frequently involves getting to know each
other as they go through the experience, but not always. Backwards?
Only if you think knowing the other parent of your child is important.
Before we go further, know now if your tried and true method of birth
control fails, you get to call it an "unplanned pregnancy." If you had
consensual, unprotected sex, you just consciously made a baby - period.
I could go on for pages with sarcastic remarks about people who have
unprotected sex and act shocked when a pregnancy results. This is me
holding back.

Times are changing. Some believe it is only important to know the
other parent well if you intend to stay together as a couple over the long
haul.

As a person who travels internationally for a living, I find it fascinating that the new trend in parenting, in many major cities around the free world, does not involve legal marriage.

I offer no opinion on whether this is right or wrong. I simply offer the unemotional facts. Since 2007, I have met countless couples that have a sincere desire to be parents, but since they have no reference for happiness inside of a romantic relationship, they choose not to legally marry. Some of these romantic relationships last and some do not. The relationship continues to be about parenting regardless of the romantic outcome. The theory is that the child will continue to see happy, adult relations regardless of whom their parents are romantically involved with. They sort of build an escape plan into the relationship that involves continued co-parenting. They feel that love is love and it should not matter who the partners are as long as the child sees joyful, open, loving adult relationships. These people believe they are more intelligent than their parents who suffered through unhappy marriages for their children. My Auntie Juanna is spinning in her grave, no doubt, but this is becoming a very popular attitude.

Interestingly, if you think about it, this is potentially a road back to faith in committed relationships in our cultural future. If this works, the children of these anarchists will indeed see that love is a safe and beautiful thing and theoretically, they will carry on an attitude of comfort in the arena of commitment and loving relations. Hey, it could happen. Then we have some cultures where it is tradition for the man to "spread his seed" with as many women as possible. This is strange, but true. These men leave most of the child rearing to the ladies and show up for what they deem "important events" and share their "wisdom" as the child grows.

Other Baby Makers from the old days were women who tried to get pregnant to trap men into marriage. That doesn't work any more. So now, ladies who want a baby just have unprotected sex and hope for healthy fertilization. They will make babies without consulting with their lovers simply because they want to be mothers.

If this freaks you out, guys, WEAR A CONDOM. Hello! This is not brain surgery.

Ladies, if you don't like the idea of your lover "spreading his seed" and not committing, MAKE HIM WEAR A CONDOM. Hello! Again, not brain surgery.

Last, we have couples that fall in love, get married, talk things through, and start a family. Wow. You guys are old fashioned! Perhaps the last of a dying breed, but I applaud your romanticism, dedication, and commitment. As I sit on a plane headed for Maui, the land of just-say-no-to-commitment, I think how different you guys are. Not better, not worse, just different.

You are the biggest risk takers of the Baby Maker group.
In conclusion, Baby Makers come in all sizes, shapes and motivations. As with many of our Couple Personality Types, Baby Makers really should date each other. Unlike the other Types, there are serious long-term consequences that need to be considered.

As a writer and as a woman, I urge you to discuss your long term plans with your lover and make sure everyone is on the same page with this one. Parenting is the ultimate commitment, so be responsible.

Part 8

Jacob was there as soon as I walked in to the waiting room. He had already checked with the paramedics and found out a few details. He just grabbed me and held on for a minute.

Sheila and Eric were also there. They told me that it was a pretty bad accident. Someone hadn't been paying attention and ran a red light. They smashed into Brad's car, thankfully, on the rear passenger side and not a classic T-Bone. His car was totaled and was hauled away. We did know that he hit his steering wheel pretty hard with his chest and was being x-rayed. We'd know more, later.

I hugged them all and stormed over to the nurse's station and demanded to know when I could see him.

"Calm down, ma'am," the attending nurse said. I didn't even care this time. Damned, skippy, I'm a ma'am. And don't you forget it. Now, I want some fricking service! But, instead, again with the sugar ants...

"Darling, pardon my pushiness, it's just that he called me from the scene of the accident. He wants to see me."

I felt Eric behind me now.

"Are you family?" the nurse asked calmly.

I looked at Eric and he just smiled and raised an eyebrow. I could feel my throat start to tighten and my eyes burn. I stood for what seemed like an eternity before I turned around and responded.

"Yes, I am. My name is Sarina Stone, and that man is my fiancé."

It was three hours later before the doctor came to the waiting room. She explained that Brad had some broken and some bruised ribs, but he would be just fine. They checked thoroughly to be sure no fragments pierced his lungs, and that's what took so long. He told us there would be more tests, but they were standard and simple. Eric excused himself to go make arrangements in case he was doing the show solo tomorrow. Sheila said she was almost finished balancing out the energy around Brad and would call later. Jacob hugged me and said he'd be right there and off I went.

I had it all planned out. This man needed to hear how much I love him. He needed to know he wasn't alone and that I was there for him. He needed me.

I entered Brad's room. Apparently, what he needed more than me was sleep, because that's what he was doing when I walked in. I took a sharp breath in when I saw him. He looked so weak and pale. Almost immediately, two male orderlies came in and said they needed to take him for another test. It would be less than an hour. They eased his unconscious body on to a table-like bed with wheels and invited me to wait in his room. It made me weak with helplessness to see him wheeled away.

Maybe it was the intensity of the moment, or maybe it was the chemicals floating in that hospital air, but something happened. It hit me like a ton of bricks. I felt sick and dizzy. My head began to pound. I tried to reach for the empty bed, but staggered as the room began to fade to deep purple, then dark gray and the bed disappeared. Then it got weird.

If I had to put a visual to it, I would say it was like a spike of knowledge slammed into my crown and penetrated my brain. Time ceased to be linear. I experienced it as a pinprick of a moment in which the beginning, middle and end of a story was experienced and understood.

I saw the whole thing in a flash – Brad, Jacob, even Gary. It was like the story had already been written and I was playing my part. The lesson was delivered simultaneously with the episode that inspired it. It wasn't in fast motion; it was a split second in which I experienced months of interactions and emotions. I felt, rather than saw who I was with each of the men in my life. I felt how my energy shifted from relationship to relationship and how this shift affected the field around me. I knew in an instant who each of us was and what our energetic relationship was to each other. I could feel our past, present, and future's as soul buddies. There was a deep understanding of the roles each of us played in this lifetime and how we bring sacred messages and opportunities for growth to each other.

I saw Jacob and felt how deeply he allowed my opinions and actions affect him. Our relationship seemed to span time itself and is impossible to explain. I did not see us in what may be perceived as past lives, rather I felt him as I felt my own skin today. I felt his watchful eye and energetic aura of protection around me for millennia and beyond. Jacob was and is my defender and confidant. He always has been and always will be.

There were multiple scenarios with Gary. What I saw with him was different than Jacob. I saw the two of us in lifetime after lifetime together (either that or I have some bizarre costuming issues in my visions now). We were always a couple; always impassioned. No wonder I couldn't resist him – we went way back. I knew his touch like I know my own. I saw that each decision I made in this life affected an outcome, but all roads led to enlightenment with Gary; some roads were simply easier than others. Gary taught me about being at peace with femininity and keeping my integrity.

And Brad, he was there. He was a part of the crazy mix. Every word, every thought I carried touched him. I saw how accepting he was in this life and realized that I was one of the messengers who brought him this internal strength. I saw other lives with him where we switched roles as teacher, student, father, and mother. His love for me was stronger than his disappointment every time. Brad taught me compassion and patience.

I got it. It all made sense. The gifts they gave to me paralleled the gifts I gave to them. We were all part of the same moving, breathing, consciousness, and yet, completely unique as conscious beings.

Connected by the Source and connected to each other, we spun through time and rode the waves of possibility like the adventuresome spirits we were. I saw it. I felt it...

And then, it was over. Just like that, I was aware of my surroundings again. In the blink of an eye, the rush of knowledge stopped and I was experiencing myself and time in a nice, normal, linear fashion. All I could say was "What the..."

It took me a second to get my bearings. I literally pinched myself to make sure I wasn't dreaming. I needed to sit down. I took one more step toward the bed and a second wave of energy hit me and I gasped as a new flood of memories filled my mind. This time they came the good old fashioned way, slow, linear, and confronting as hell.

Images of me rejecting Brad in numerous ways bombarded me. I remembered them all, but this time I could feel Brad's spirit break as I spat cruel words and broke his trust. I relived all the cups of coffee, drawn baths, and occasion-less flowers he gave me. Worst, I felt his joy when giving me an engagement ring and the agony when I blew off the idea of a wedding.

I saw what I was committed to. I saw how that internal commitment had nothing to do with the verbal commitment I made to this man. I saw the lengths I went to in order to stay congruent with my screwed up need for space.

It seemed to go on and on - one ugly, insensitive scene after another. The shame was palpable. I sort of reeled over to Brad's bed. Perhaps it was just impossible to focus on the visions in my mind and the physical act of falling at the same time, but I swear it was like I was moving through molasses as I went down, totally slow motion. I slowly came to my knees at the edge of the bed, like I was a little kid saying my prayers before I went to sleep. I held my head, shut my eyes, and waited for the horrible visions to stop. Which, thank God, eventually they did.

My eyes were held shut and I stayed in that prayer position waiting for the next slap in the face, blood pounding in my ears. Eventually, blackness overtook me and I drifted off to a place of nothingness.

"Ma'am? Ma'am, are you ok?"

"Huh?" I choked.

"I couldn't tell if you were praying or sleeping. Seeing someone we love in the hospital can be shocking. I just wanted to be sure you were alright."

I looked up and saw a twelve-year-old in one of those candy striped outfits I'd seen on TV. Her badge said 'Hi. My name is Tami.'

Tami helped me up and walked me over to a chair in the corner of the room. She poured me a cup of water and handed it to me with a look that clearly relayed that not drinking was not an option. The moment the cool liquid hit my mouth I spat it out. Unfortunately, Tami was in the trajectory and got nailed.

"Ugh! What the heck is that stuff?" I hissed.

"It's water, ma'am."

"Where did you get it?"

"I just filled this pitcher up in the kitchen," she said.

"Well, it tastes like ass. You people should know better. The patient needs clean, filtered water. Don't you dare give this to Brad when…"

I tried to stand up and collapsed onto Tami. She caught me and helped me sit back down.

"I'm going to call a doctor for you," she said.

"No. Please. I'm fine now. I just need a minute to collect myself. Like you said, it's all just so shocking."

At that moment, Tami's pager went off. It must have been important because she agreed to let me sit there, wait for Brad, and rest until she got back. I actually did sit for a while and tried to put it all together. Just when I get used to my whacked out visions, they get upgraded to a whole new breed. My little gift was evolving and I was trying to hang on for the ride.

I could feel my strength returning after a few minutes. My mind was clearing, too. What I really wanted was a glass of fresh, clean water. And that would require moving. Funny to think I'd get cleaner water at a gas station quick mart than at the hospital. By funny, I mean sick.

I wasn't sure what I was going to do to win Brad back, but I definitely knew what I needed to do with Mister Gary Parker. If I did it right, I could get everything handled before Brad even missed me.
This time when I stood up, I only teetered a little bit. I took a deep breath and walked over to Brad's still empty bed, and kissed his pillow. Making sure reddish pink lips remained imprinted on the white pillow case, I smiled and left the empty room.

Out in the waiting area, my sweet Jacob was passed out in a chair. I swear that man could sleep anywhere. I wrote a note and stuck it on his lap.

It read:
Jacob,
Please forgive the transgressions of the past few days. I'm cleaning that up right now.
Thanks for being here for Brad, and me.
Sarina

I went to my car and drove straight to the Grand Hotel. Fifteen minutes later, I was knocking on Gary Parker's door. Thank God, he didn't answer. I mean, what did I think I was going to say? Whew.

I was completely lost in my own thoughts when I turned the corner to head for the elevator and, you won't believe this, smacked right in to him. Okay, no one bumps into that many people in two days. This was getting surreal. I was thinking I should start wearing hockey gear or something.

Thank goodness we didn't have anything in our hands, so we just sort of staggered back a step or two and stopped to look at each other for a moment. Then, Gary smiled and was almost child-like when he realized it was me.

"Hey, beautiful. I was just thinking about you!" he beamed. "You come to see me?"

"Yes?"

"Then you're taking me up on my offer and spending some time with me tonight?" And before I could say anything, big Gary Parker swept me up in his very powerful arms, pulled me close and kissed me. This time, I didn't kiss back.

He stepped away and just looked at me. "Did I miss something? I thought we made a connection."

"We did," I said heading back to his room. "Can we talk?"

Gary's room was really nice in the late afternoon light. It had obviously been cleaned and the décor was early American wealthy - my favorite.

"I'm not in the habit of throwing myself at women who doesn't want me, Sarina. So, let's get this out."

"Last night, I was single. Today, I'm not." Oh, that was brilliant.

You're a professional writer and a public speaker, and that's the best you could come up with? Plus, I ended that last sentence with a preposition. So, sue me.

"Gary," I continued, "what I mean is that when I met you, I seriously believed I had finished with the man I'd been living with."

"You're living with someone?"

"Right now, it's Jacob."

"You're living with Jacob?" Now Gary was a little red in the face.

As always, I started laughing in the wrong place and the wrong time (I've been kicked out of two restaurants and a poetry reading for that. But those are different stories).

Gary stood up and headed for the door. "I'll do my best not to let this effect your contract, but you are definitely not what I thought I was signing on for. Wow. You are a great actor, you had me fooled."

"Wait," I shouted as he opened the door for me to leave. "I'm just crashing at Jacob's while I work things out with my fiancé."

The moment I said it, I wanted to take it back. Gary's face was actually contorted now. I thought he was going to snap.

"You're engaged?"

"Uh, sort of. If he'll have me."

"What the hell does that mean?" he said calming a little.

"Why don't you close the door and I'll tell you all about it," I said. "It's actually sort of funny."

I don't think either one of us bought into the funny thing, but Gary did close the door and I did spend the next half hour explaining everything.

I started out by explaining to Gary that I believe that sometimes we meet people for a reason. In this case, based on results, we were drawn together to learn something about ourselves at the very least. At the very most, it felt as though we were already trusted friends (even though I tried to deny it). I suppose that wouldn't have worked if he had not believed in something beyond this reality, but he did and he agreed that there was something unexplainable between us. It was like we knew each other already, and not just because he had done his research on my show. It went a lot deeper than that.

I'm not one who brings spirituality into common conversation, but if two people ever had a "connection," it was Gary and I. I guess I just wanted Gary to know that I had nothing but respect for the relationship we had, new as it may be.

We talked more about him, too. Turns out, Mr. Parker never gets personal with his colleagues. The energetic bond between us swept him away. He knew exactly who I was and invited me to spend the night anyway. Smooth move.

And, me? I knew that Brad and I were just fighting. It's not my style to use a lame excuse to allow myself anything. The only difference between us was that I had a commitment to another man, and Gary, well he wanted to remain swept away a while longer.

At the end of it all, he apologized for cracking the sexual innuendo jokes over lunch and made sure I knew he would never use sex as a means to secure a deal. I told him I was flattered, and in different circumstances, I thought we'd be a great couple. Hopefully, we would be great business associates and some day, maybe, good friends.

"I'd really appreciate it if this stayed between us," I said.

"You're not telling your fiancé?"

"I mean, in the press. Brad and I will go public when we're ready. I just want to be sure, that's all."

"Uh- huh. Again, will you be telling your future husband you had fantastic sex with a stranger last night, Miss Couple Chat?"

"I don't know. Did I mention that he's heavily sedated in a hospital bed right now, Gary? Did I mention that when he called from the accident I let it go to voice mail?"

"Oh, my God. You didn't tell me," he almost shouted. "Is he okay?"

"Yeah. He's going to be fine." I started to grab my purse and stand up. "But, I'm sure you understand that I can't stay."

"Of course," he said moving toward the door. "So, I suppose I shouldn't kiss you goodbye."

"Uh, no."

Gary opened the heavy oak door. "And a blowjob is out of the question?"

We both laughed at that. Gary and I hugged for what seemed like minutes. We still felt that spark. But this time I was an adult about it and followed my ethics instead of my hormones. So, I kissed him on the cheek and off I went, back to the hospital to see Brad and beg him to forgive my horrible behavior and give us another try. At least that's what I thought I was going to do...

Only Children Couples

Only : an adverb used to indicate the one thing or person that solely or exclusively happens or is involved in a situation after the one mentioned

1.   (Adj) used to indicate the single person or thing involved in a situation
2.   (Adj) with no brothers or sisters
      Children: Plural of child

Encarta® World English Dictionary © 1999 Microsoft Corporation. All rights reserved. Developed for Microsoft by Bloomsbury Publishing Plc.

> *"If you realize that all things change, there is nothing you will try to hold on to."*
> *-Laozi*

More and more these days we see older people (people over 35) stepping into the arena of Commitment for the first time. Now, what we have here are mature adults who have been living on their own for years, trying to share not only their lives, but also at times, their stuff with someone else. It's totally different when a young person with little life experience partners with someone. There is no lifestyle to compromise. But, when a person has grown accustomed to doing laundry on Wednesday and putting their keys on the mantle, it can be confronting when someone else, with different habits, comes strolling into the house and touches their stuff.

I call these folks Only Children Couples because your classic only children have little or no experience with other people touching their stuff as they grew up. Unlike the children of multi-child households where little was sacred and most people had limited privacy, much less ownership of their stuff, the Only Children were the kings and queens of their domains. Chances are, mom or dad never came in and just started playing with their toys uninvited. They probably never had someone break or remove their toys. They went to the bathroom when they felt like it because their parents had their own bathroom. They did not share their toys unless they were entertaining. Even entertaining could be calculated as toys that were "hands-off" could be removed prior to company arriving. Yes, the only child knew little of the stress of people touching their stuff or other irritating inconveniences that children with siblings household did. When only children grow up, they tend to have systems for pretty much everything. These systems depend on calculated behaviors and dedication to performing certain tasks in a certain way, often at certain times. If someone comes along and starts touching their stuff, moving things around or disturbing the natural order of things, extreme discomfort ensues.

So, our Only Children Couples are people who sincerely want to be together, but actually find the experience of sharing physical things or responsibility unnatural and uncomfortable. This discomfort with sharing can actually turn very sweet couples into Fighter Couples. Again, I had to get out there and interview people on the subject. I found that like the Baby Makers Couples, there actually are new trends with those fiercely independent mature couples that feel comfortable with committing to intimacy, but are not comfortable with cohabitation, or sharing responsibility or stuff.

There are two ways to do this. One is to get your behinds into counseling and learn to share your toys. Learn to focus on what is there that is beautiful. Learn to turn a blind eye to the fact that you know you put your keys on the mantle and now there is a bouquet of flowers there and although the keys are gone, your partner swears there was nothing on there when they brought the flowers home. Yes, there is a way to do this, but the old dog is gonna have to learn some new tricks.

The second way Only Children Couples are dealing with each other is to have separate residences. They tell me they enjoy having sleepovers. They also enjoy going back to their respective places and having private time. These couples tell me it's like having their cake and eating it, too. Of course, this means the couple can afford it, and they trust each other enough not to have to spend every night together. A variation of this last lifestyle choice is to create separate spaces inside of one living space. Her studio, his den, etc. This does not guarantee that

our Only Child Couple will not step on the occasional toe, but it certainly shows dedication and commitment to being a creative, committed couple.

Part 9

I walked in to the hospital and found Jacob in Brad's room. Brad was sleeping with a pillow blocking the light from his face. I had a HUGE bouquet of colorful flowers and handed them to Jacob.

"You want me to put these in water?" he asked.

"Do what you want," I said "They're for you."

I knew Jacob got it. We'd been together too long for him not to. I was saying, "I'm sorry." There's nothing like $100 worth of gorgeous flowers to make a statement.

"Has he been up?" I asked.

"Yes, off and on," Jacob replied, "he was asking for you."

"Jacob," I said with my most serious whisper, "I really screwed things up with Brad. I'm going to beg him for forgiveness as soon as he wakes up." I was whispering fast now. "I just need to tell him what an ass I've been and I know everything will be okay. I mean, he'll forgive me, won't he? I know everything will be okay. It has to be."

I was losing it. I thought I knew what I wanted, but now that I was here, I was filled with doubt – and my best buddy could see it. Shit. Did it ever end? Why couldn't I make up my fricking mind? Why couldn't I stop shaking? Love wasn't supposed to be this hard.

"Actually," Jacob broke my thoughts by whispering very quietly in my

ear, "I don't care who you end up with. I want you to be happy."
"What the hell are you talking about?" I damned near shouted. Brad
stirred a little and I looked down, but he became still again. I couldn't
see his face because of the light shielding pillow. Jacob was just
staring at me.
I bent over and whispered in Jacob's ear. "Who I end up with?"

"Okay, play dumb," he said "I just want to be sure this story ends with
an empty guest room. Namely, mine." Jacob kissed my cheek. "The
doc says he's going to be fine. You want me to stay?"

"No," I said focusing back on Brad, "I've got it from here."
He held his bouquet and took a big sniff. Then he smiled and headed
for the door. Before he passed over the threshold he stopped for a
moment with his back to me.

"What? I said.
Jacob turned around, "Just because something you do pisses me off,
doesn't mean it's actually bad. I just wanted you to know that I'm
aware of these things."

I had no idea what he was talking about, but I smiled and nodded like a
Thai taxi driver.

I turned my full focus on to sleeping Brad. I was going to be there
when that man woke up. This was the beginning of a new Sarina. I
was gonna be the picture of domestication. That's right, look out
world, Sarina Stone is, oh, hey, look, over there, something shiny.

No really, on the floor by the chair was something shiny. I walked
over to it and picked it up. It was a perfect little black diamond
cufflink. I must have scooped it up with my jewelry this morning and
shoved it in my pocketbook. Now it had fallen out and I bent over to
pick it up.

It was understated, this piece of man-jewelry. Only a trained eye
would know these were diamonds. I have such an eye. I stood for

a moment, with my back to the hospital bed and just marveled at the sheer artistry of this object. From that thought, my mind went to other details of the previous evening. Crystal glasses, soft bath towels, Italian tile, and a feather bed. Such attention to detail; such delight in the artistry of every day living; such presence.

"Honey," Brad croaked softly as he started to unveil his face from behind the pillow, "is that you?"

Part 10

Ten days later I could not stop crying. This was starting be ridiculous. "Love shouldn't be this hard," Brad said to me when I started to plead my wait-for-marriage case a few days ago. "We both deserve to be in love, Sarina. You know I'm right on this one, honey. There's just something missing between us."

That was the beginning of this three-day break up talk. This time Brad agreed that we shouldn't get married. He said that it wasn't right. He agreed with everything I said, and I didn't know how to handle it. There was nothing to push against, he was 100% compliant, 100% confident and 100% sure that he had had enough.

I sniffed, "It's just that this seems so permanent. You've been such a big part of my life for so long..."

Brad and I had done some serious soul searching in the days since his accident. What I can explain is why I love Brad. He is kind, gentle, generous, and extremely smart. He knows me and likes me anyway. He is not at all swayed by my public personality. He's my biggest fan and supports me in all that I strive to accomplish – professional and otherwise.

What I can't explain is why this isn't enough for me to fall in love. I loved Brad, but it was clear to us both that the type of affection I felt for him was more sisterly than it should be. I honestly didn't get the difference between these two loves until now. In Iceland, there are different words for different loves. In America, we use the same word for our love for food as we use for out love for a sibling, color, or romantic partner. But, there is a difference, and this difference is huge and makes absolutely no sense most of the time. I mean, I'd be the luckiest girl in the world if Brad made my heart twitter.

I also cannot tell you why I chose to live with Brad and push him away when he showed affection. That was ridiculous. I still squirm a little with discomfort at the thought of it. I am a very lucky girl that this man sees a good person underneath my crappy avoidance behavior.

In the end, Brad was the smart, no-nonsense man I grew to love. His accident made him appreciate each moment he had on this planet. He chose not to waste it chasing a woman who clearly wasn't into him. Brad let me go with all the love and grace of an angel. He never judged me. He never accused me of being cold or mean (both of which I was at certain points in our relationship).

I think what impressed me the most was his shift in commitment. Brad changed after the accident. All he wanted was to be happy. In order for that to occur for him, he needed open, loving connections with those he was close to. He was sick of chasing unattainable goals. He was committed to accepting the people in his life unconditionally. This meant he didn't ask the plumber to do brain surgery and then act disappointed when they didn't deliver. He wanted a lover who missed him when he was gone and cherished the moments they had together. That's not asking too much, and he just figured that out.

I don't miss anyone. It's not good or bad, it just is. Well, I once had a Rottweiler. I missed him if I was away for more than a week or two. I tattooed his name on my shoulder after he died; maybe that counts. When I said, "I guess I should start moving my stuff out," he didn't skip a beat. He simply agreed with a weak smile. Such strength.

I realize, in retrospect, that all he was waiting for was for me to fight for us – for him. When I didn't, he was finished. Simple and adult.

"I'm sure Jacob can put you up while you apartment hunt," he said. Then, "Or, you could always stay with your mom."

It was the first time we laughed together in a long time. It was such a quick, short ending to our long cherished relationship. After three days of talks, we decided cold turkey was the way to go. We agreed that I should move right away. We agreed on everything and somehow that made it the hurt cut deeper.

Eventually, I kissed Brad on the cheek and went to the bedroom, his bedroom, to pack my things.

"Hey, it's me." I said as was folding a little Jil Sander skirt. I was holding the phone between my ear and shoulder. "I'm moving out." Pause. "No, this time it's for good. I'm okay, really. It's the right thing. Jacob, I'd really appreciate it if I could crash at your place while I apartment hunt." Another pause. "Yeah, I heard. Rah team. Let's announce it on the show tomorrow. See you in a few."

I hung up, finished packing, and started walking out of Brad's apartment while he was in the kitchen. I know he purposefully stayed in there so I could make an un-dramatic exit and save a little face if I wanted to. I wanted to.

The next day was Eric's last day in Minnesota and last episode of Couple Chat for a while. I barely spent any time with him, but somehow he was one of the pillars that kept me going these past few days.

I opened the show the same way I always did.

"Welcome to Couple Chat. I'm Sarina Stone." Then, in my slinkiest, sexiest, most soothing voice, "So, fellow Tao-bots, here's some special news about your favorite radio host. First, now you can travel safe knowing that you can listen to Couple Chat in every major city in America. That's right, we're officially syndicated. I know this elates and inspires you all." I chuckled as I said this last part. "You'll also be able to catch us on television soon. I don't want to jinx it completely, so I'll just say that a very famous celebrity with a very famous day-time talk show has invited us for an interview. I can't say who she is but her name rhymes with Opera."

Jacob rolled his eyes so far to the back of his head, they got stuck there for a second.

"Last," I crooned, "I have finally decided to write a book for the guys. That's right lover, Why Real Men Drink Straight Tequila – The Tao of Chivalry, is under way as we speak."

"Anyone helping with that, Miss Stone?" Eric chimed in.
"Why yes, Mr. Thurnbeck. I think your listeners are going to be very pleased..."

The phone lines lit up instantly. Call after call from men wanting to talk. Guys either wanted to encourage Eric or ask advice on the spot. The minutes flew by and we finally went to commercial.

Once it became quiet, I was so moved, I could barely speak – which was good, because no one expected me to; at least not for another four minutes.

Epilogue

Six weeks later

I had two weeks left at Jacob's, and then I would be moving to a darling little flat in the Uptown area of Minneapolis. Jacob found this great place with hard wood floors and a built-in oak buffet, just blocks from Lake of the Isles. It was a real find, and I was looking forward to moving in. Jacob was a great guy, but we both needed our privacy. From my little desk in Jacob's guestroom, I could see that he was cooking. There was a steak, broccoli and mushrooms on the counter. "Are you expecting a hot date?" I shouted.

"Wouldn't you like to know?" He grinned and kept puttering.
He must have been expecting company. He tidied the living room and
even lit incense. I was just about to get up and interrogate when my
phone rang. I recognized the number and picked up.

"Yes, I'd like a cheese pizza with an extra thin crust please." I said.

"Would you like a drink with that, ma'am? A decaf, soy miel,
perhaps?"
Oh, he was good.

"Hi Gary. What's going on?" I said, surprised at how happy I was to
hear his voice.

"Have I waited long enough to be considered sensitive and
appropriate?" he asked.

"What do you mean?" I said. "Waited for what?"

"Waited to tell you that I can't stop thinking about you."

I was floored. This is what Jacob was talking about that day at the
hospital. He knew. He knew that Gary Parker and I had "something"
between us that had nothing to do with anonymous sex or work. And
now, here he was, on my phone, whispering sweet nothings.

"Hello? You still there?" he blurted.

"Uh, yeah. Yeah. I'm here. I'm just digesting."

"That's gross. I love that about you." He said and I could hear him
smiling.

"You can't stop thinking about me. You don't mean this
professionally, do you?"

"No." he said. "I just wanted to wait until you were over the big break up. Are you okay now?"

"Yeah, the whole 'dark night of the soul' thing only lasted a few weeks. I'm a little wobbly, but I'm pretty ok. I found an apartment. I'm looking forward to that."

"So, you're still at Jacob's?"

"Yep. Two more weeks "

"So, if you felt like going to Blue for a cocktail, you could be there in minutes?"

"I suppose so." I answered.

"Then, I think you should." He said in a low, slinky tone. "There's someone there who can't wait to hold you in his arms."

I was shaking now. He was so forward. He didn't even play the sex card. He played hearts.

"Are you here? I mean, in Minnesota?" I blurted.

"Would you like me to be?"

"Well, it would be pretty weird if someone besides you was waiting for me, like the doorman or someone."

"Do you miss me, Sarina?"

No misdirection tonight.

"Maybe." I teased, but I know he could hear me smiling.

"Then, maybe I'm just a mile away." He said. "Maybe I was on my way back to New York and I stopped over in Minneapolis just hoping you wanted to see me. Maybe I came to the Grand Hotel because that's where I think I left my heart."

I could not speak. It's rare, but it happens.

"Please say something," he said, "I'm pouring my heart out here."

"I know. I just need a minute."

"Then take a minute. Get dressed and come to Blue. Nothing will happen that you don't invite. I just want to see you outside of a business meeting, Sarina. God, I feel like I'm going crazy…"

"I-I-I don't know what to say." I stuttered.

"Say you'll come."

Twenty minutes later, I walked into the kitchen to find Jacob slicing mushrooms in silence. The house looked great. I did, too. No girl yet, but I saw two place settings on the table.

"Wow. Where are you going?" he asked.

"Believe it or not, Mr. GP just called. He made a stop-over in Minnesota to see me."

"We have a meeting?"

"Uh, no."

"You have a meeting?"

"Uh, no."

"Okay, I'll play your silly game. What's going on?"

"He can't stop thinking about me." Then I looked at Jacob and dropped my smile. "You said a relationship with him would piss you off."

"I also told you that just because it pissed me off, doesn't mean it's wrong."

Yet another priceless moment of silence this evening.

"So?" Jacob chirped. "What are you waiting for?"

"Oddly enough, your blessing." I said.

"Consider yourself blessed." He said with a silly flourish brandishing a piece of broccoli, like a sword or magic wand. I had to laugh -partially out of relief, and partially because he's a very funny man.

"All right. Well, now you have privacy, which is probably what you really wanted tonight."

"I love it when I get what I want." He said. "Now get out of here."

I hugged Jacob so tightly, he was taken aback. Then, I left and headed out for my next adventure – LOVE.

Fifteen minutes later

Jacob was pulling a steak out of the broiler. He had gorgeous steamed veggies in a bowl on the kitchen counter. He set the broiler pan on top of the stove and went to the dining table. Jacob removed the second setting. He placed the dish back in the cupboard, replaced the silverware in its drawer, and set the glass on its shelf.

He placed the steak on a serving platter and brought it and the veggies to the table. He went back for a glass of iced tea and some garlic salt. Once at the table, Jacob quietly served himself the sumptuous meal and took a bite. Delicious. He checked his watch and picked up the TV remote. The Channel Five news was on. "This would be a great time for the rumor mill to be accurate," he thought to himself as he raised the volume.

"...next, Minnesota is proud to congratulate home town radio personality and author, Sarina Stone. Today, GP Enterprises announced that negotiations were in play for the production of the film, Why Real Couples Drink Straight Tequila, based on the popular book by our own Sarina Stone. It is speculated that this feature film will be made right here, in the Twin Cities. Congratulations, Sarina."

Jacob took a large bite of his juicy steak and chewed like the cat that swallowed the canary. In a few seconds, the smirk was glazed over by silent, welling, tears. It was the end of an era - and the beginning of another.

"Take the leap, Tao sister, take the leap."

THE END

Chapter 8

Information and Stories From
Amazing People About Real
Relationships and Commitment

Selection 1

Past Life Relationships and Their Effect on the Present Day - How Deep Is Your Soul?

by Rev. Sheila Van Houten, DD, PhD

And now for something a little different…

In my experience as a personal coach, one of the things that will make a person sick is the inability to either forget or understand an attraction to another person. Sometimes we meet someone and it really feels like we've known him or her forever. If you are lucky, the connection feels good and all is well. But, sometimes the relationship is unhealthy and we just can't shake the connection. Perfectly stable people become obsessed and ultimately crumble when this occurs. When this happens, some people call my friend Sheila.

Sheila has a gift. She can help track a relationship back to its origin, usually not in this lifetime, and explain what the circumstances by which the dynamics were created. I know it sounds crazy, but many people have come to understand their feelings toward another by learning how it all began.

I have asked Sheila to write a piece about this phenomenon

because it applies to so many of us.

"Quantum energy can exist in two very different forms: as visible particles, or invisible waves. A quantum particle can be in one place only, two places at once, or even many places simultaneously." (Source: See Footnote.)

What are you made of?

You are made of energy in the form of waves and particles. That means you can be visible and invisible, both at the same time. That means you can even be in one or more locations at the same time.

Aren't you amazing?[1]

Let's process this amazement a bit! Here's how we can start:

Today I had one of those flash-back experiences that put me into a tailspin of nostalgia. I believe you will relate.

For no particular reason that I can think of, I was suddenly transported back in time, and I saw myself in my beautiful strapless, white prom dress, complete with bustle and hoop, excitedly hurrying down the sidewalk in the old neighborhood to my best friend's house for "coketails".

I was looking forward to seeing my high school sweetheart in his Navy uniform. He was on his way home on leave in exactly one hour, just in time for this most important life event! At seventeen, what could possibly be better for me?

I can still feel the warmth of the setting sun on my face. I can still feel the delight I felt that everything was going just absolutely splendidly. It was a moment of bliss – pure bliss.

---

1   Quote Source: The Spontaneous Healing of Belief (page 11) by Greg Braden

It seemed to have happened five minutes ago instead of decades ago.

When I came back to the present and thought of how much time had elapsed since that evening, I got a feeling of utter panic and a sense of profound loss. The whole reverie triggered a bizarre sort of brain hiccup, and I felt slightly dizzy. I felt like I was free falling. I felt lost in space, suspended in time.

After I recovered my equilibrium, I began to wonder, and not for the first time either, about the nature of time itself and what might be the truth about it.

It is said by some that everything takes place all at once: the past, the present, and the future. How confounding that idea is to us, who are so linearly fixated, so left-brained and logic- oriented. How could it possibly be that way?

Yet, if we were to take up a perch way out in outer space and view our little lives from that perspective, we might see that everything IS taking place in an instant and all at the same time. It is only when we are stuck on the ground; captives of gravity; that we feel like time is moving at a snail's pace.

Another rather strange idea out there is that we have multiple parallel lives going on at the same time. How can this be? Let's follow this thread, suspend judgment, and see where we can go with it. Let's say that we do have lives in other dimensions going on right now, and then let's say that we have past, present, and future lives going on as well, right now.

All of these lives can create what I think of as "bleed through", much like my nostalgic recall of prom night, so that we can suddenly become gripped by an inexplicable emotion or thought because it is actually happening somewhere else! Right now!

No wonder we are a brew of roiling emotion! Some are more aware of this roiling emotion than others, and they are called empaths. Some try to ignore or hide from this roiling emotion, and they are called insensitives. Regardless, the brew remains.

Many folks also assert that we came here from other dimensions where we could create outcomes in the blink of a thought, and that is why the lesson of patience is such a universal given on this beautiful planet of ours. We inherently know how to create instantly, but here, it doesn't work that way!

Time and time again, we are hurled to the ground in our attempts to create an instant anything! As a friend of mine says about life on planet earth, "You don't get it all, and you don't get it all at once!"

Here is another astounding idea from quantum physics. This one has been proven over and over again, too. It goes like this: anything that was once connected always behaves if it were still connected. It is the waves and particles again, the stuff we are all made of. In that sense, we are all one, all connected, and all made of the same-stuff.

That same-stuff fact accounts for at least two different corollaries: Racial memory: We already "remember and know everything" on a subconscious level and the 100th monkey phenomenon: 99 monkeys are washing their potatoes on island #1. On another island, island #2, the monkeys are not washing their potatoes. Through a form of mental telepathy, the 100th monkey on island #2 gets the message to wash his potato too, and does. Soon, all the other monkeys on his island start doing it as well. Now we have two islands of monkeys washing their potatoes without any face-to-face communication having taken place.

Let us have a closer look at this fact of connectedness. There are mind-bending experiments to prove it. The simplest one is the DNA samples in a jar.

Human test subjects were swabbed for DNA. Then, the DNA was put into solution in a jar and moved to a different room. The subjects were submitted to both positive and negative experiences. The DNA was observed for responses.

The DNA exhibited organized, graceful movement when it was

given positive stimuli and jagged, random, disorganized movement when it was exposed to negative stimuli. These were replicated experiments, meaning the same results happened over and over again.

Perhaps more popularly known is the work done by Dr. Masaru Emoto. He did a similar kind of experiment with frozen water crystals. In fact, he created a wonderful collection of crystals that were photographed as perfectly gorgeous when subjected to happy words on pieces of paper and ugly and distorted when subjected to negative words!

To summarize, quantum physics has given us some truths we can take some comfort in. Those truths are these:

We are capable of being in different dimensions at the same time,

We are capable of being visible and invisible at the same time,

We are not confined to this gravity-ruled planet; we are, in fact, free, and yet, paradoxically, we are all connected because we are all made of the same stuff!

Think of the possibilities!

Think of how archaic an airplane flight becomes when you consider the probability of instant, even simultaneous travels! No wonder I refuse to fly the friendly skies of the airline industry! To me, it's as primitive as the covered wagon! Maybe it's even worse. At least with a covered wagon, you could stop and get out at will.

Who knows? You might be having three major love affairs, or even a hundred, all at the same time right now! You might be soaring in the skies over the Pacific Ocean in one of your lives and dining on Sushi in Shanghai in another right now! The possibilities are endless! Think of the connections; the relationships; the sex!

Now consider this: when you are momentarily back in the body and your conscious mind is operating, you could even have magnificent recollections of everything you have been up to in all those dimensions on any particular day!

Could that be what your "imagination" really is: A series of recollections? Could it be that your dreams really are actual experiences in different dimensions?

That brings me to my centerpiece idea: The main reason why we feel attraction toward one person and revulsion toward another is that we are all interconnected through all of our various personas and existences and our very DNA. If we have mixed feelings about another, it could be because we have mixed roles going on in our various locations, or a racial memory about that person!

I haven't even mentioned yet the complexities of the past-life connections we all have, and the unfinished business from those connections. It seems we bring in with us a host of unfinished karmic relationships that cause us to have strange and often compulsive attractions for certain people, or certain types of people with certain types of relational dynamics. For instance, you simply cannot get Donald or Linda out of your psyche no matter how hard you try, and even though the relationship isn't working, or is painful, or is part of a repeating pattern of frustration, you go back and back and back to it.

If you are sick and tired of all of that, consider past-life regression, and consider contacting me to help you with it. I specialize in past-life regression, and I have never once in my entire career had anyone find it any less than miraculous in resolving relationship and life issues. That's quite a statement, isn't it? I have seen peculiar physical and emotional disturbances just up and disappear once the reason for them was uncovered, and I have seen destructive relationship patterns undergo dramatic improvement for the same reason. Understanding the root cause of something is often the catalyst to new behavior and the healing of old behavior. If you have troublesome relationships going on that seem to have formed a pattern, do consider unraveling your past-life connections and give me a call. I have even done these regressions right over the telephone for people in all parts of the world.

Now, here's a final zinger of a thought for you to chew on: we leave pieces of ourselves all over the place, too, and we can go around feeling less than whole until we invite these pieces back to us. A part of you may be in a past life, or on another planet, in your back yard in your current lifetime, with your father or your mother or your brother, or who knows what (or where or when, as the old song goes). If you would like some help in getting yourself back together, give me a call. I do a form of what is called "soul retrieval", and it is a very powerful process to experience, for sure a life-changing experience. You will literally be changed at a very deep level, but always for the better. There are no negatives to soul retrieval.

Do I hear you saying, "Isn't life complicated enough without all this interconnectedness going on?" The answer to that, I believe, is simply this: life is a rich tapestry that you are creating minute by minute, dimension by dimension, a matrix of existences so to speak. Do you want your tapestry to have depth and vibrancy, or do you want it to be flat and pallid? If you're after the richness, then every single experience is worthwhile in some way because you are creating your own depth as a soul. So, here's to the richness of life in all of its complexities and incomprehensibilities. Live it passionately, embrace it fully, and weave a tapestry of your own unique design. Your soul will be deep, and it will be priceless.

"Each of us is composed of all the sums he has not counted. Subtract us into nakedness and night again, and you shall see begin in Crete the love that ended yesterday in Texas."
Thomas Wolfe, The Dead Zone

Sheila's recommended reading.
"Entangled Minds", Dean Radin
"The Spontaneous Healing of Belief", Greg Braden
(Any and all books by Radin and Braden will be well worth your time and money.) "True Ghosts" by Reverend Sheila Van Houten, DD, PhD. 22 true stories that illustrate the principles of quantum physics. Contact Sheila directly for a special price.

Note: To make arrangements for a past-life regression and/or soul retrieval just give Sheila a call at 612-866-1269 or email her at achieve11@mac.com. Each experience takes about an hour. Both the past life and the soul retrieval can be done long distance or in person. Sheila audio tapes your experience so you can listen to it again later and derive new insights. It's an experience that keeps on giving.

Selection 2
Recognition

by Amy B.

I was sitting on a rickety deck in the Catskill Mountains enjoying the late afternoon summer sun. It was refreshing to leave the oppressive, hot, humid New Orleans summer for the cool, crisp, clean air of rural New York. Quiet as it was, I was excited to be attending this meditation workshop. I was finally doing something just for me; something that would further my spiritual journey. Driving up there I could not shake the feeling that I was going to meet my destiny.

I was talking to a Japanese woman from New York, over a cup of herbal tea, when Jorge, walked into my life. He sat down across from me an introduced himself,

"Hello, I'm Jorge from Puerto Rico."
I was immediately captivated.

Jorge had sparkling, rich, dark brown eyes, a generous smile, and a deep soothing voice with an incredible Spanish accent. The three of us chatted for a while about where we were from and what brought us to the workshop. Jorge's attention soon shifted as he noticed my tattoo.

My tattoo is on the inside of my right ankle; it's of a sky blue ankh with two pink roses intertwined on a green vine, one at the top and one at the bottom of the ankh. Jorge began to intensely question me about it. What did it mean? He wanted to know. I told him the story of how I had been sitting in chemistry class in the tenth grade, and had the idea of an ankh with a snake through it. A few months later, I just happened to meet someone with a tattoo gun, and I had him tattoo my leg in a friend's bedroom; I was sixteen. At the time I did not know what the symbolism of the ankh was, other than it was Egyptian in origin. My only connection to the snake was that I was born in the year of the snake according to the Chinese zodiac. Despite a fantastic drawing by my friend, the tattoo came out rather poorly since it was done by an amateur. On my eighteenth birthday, I went to a proper tattoo parlor and had the ankh re-outlined and re-shaded. The rose vine was the option to cover up the snake which now lies hidden as the vine.

In time and with more exposure to more information, the meaning of my tattoo began to evolve. I learned that the ankh symbolized eternal life. The rose is a symbol of purity and love along with being connected to many religious and ancient traditions. The snake is representative of Kundalini energy. For me, the tattoo came to mean eternal life and the will to live it, which is what I told Jorge. He said, "Oh no, there is much more to it than that." He then turned over his journal to reveal an ankh on the cover, a journal he had just purchased for the trip. I did not know then, but would soon come to find out how meaningful and powerful the tattoo was, and how it connected Jorge and me.

Jorge and I were drawn to each other. He asked if I would like to meditate in the woods with him. Feeling very relaxed and comfortable with him, I said sure. As the sun dipped below the horizon, we hiked up into the woods. We sat in the dewy grass surrounded by trees, and talked about our meditation experience. As darkness fell I felt very safe with him, though I was very much out of my element (being a city girl out in nature), and out of my normal comfort zone. We continued to gravitate toward each other, sharing every meal together, partnering up for meditation practices, and just enjoying being in each other's company. Every night we would make a cup of tea, and head out to the wooden deck and watch the fireflies light up the pitch black sky. We would then settle down inside to talk for hours. Each conversation was spent directly looking into each others eyes. Our discussions were brutally honest. We challenged each other to think of our lives from a different perspective. We laughed. Nothing was hidden; we laid our hearts, our faults, our disappointments, and our pain out for the other to see. There was this very strong sense of ease and familiarity with each other that allowed us to be bare our souls to each other.

On the third night as we sat on a wooden bridge under the twinkle of stars, I looked at Jorge seated across from me, illuminated by the moonlight and said, "I love you." He replied, "I was just about to say the same thing to you." It was not a statement of romantic love, but the acknowledgement of something deeper, something more timeless. It was the expression of the pure joy it felt to be in each other's company, the recognition that the other person was precious. It was the subconscious understanding that we knew each other on a soul level. A few mornings later Jorge was my partner for a past life regression, and while I was re-experiencing a particularly painful death, I heard his voice reach across time and space, as he gently wiped the tears from my eyes saying, "Amy, everything is okay I am right here with you." There was this sense of timelessness, that this was not the first time I had known Jorge.

The next day in another past life memory, I saw myself in Egypt, standing over a baby, my son, and I looked up into my husband's face, which I instantly recognized as Jorge. It all started to fall into place, the ankh tattoo, the connection to Egypt, and that we had been together before. During the lunch break, I raced upstairs to tell him. I looked into his eyes and I saw, saw that I had known him before. Every time I looked into his eyes I could see every lifetime we had shared reflected in them. A few months later, I was reading Journey of Souls by Michael Newton, a book about what happens to your soul when you die. The case study in the book is recalling the soul recognition class. It is a class in the spirit realm that souls attend with other souls to decide what will trigger recognition of each other in their next physical incarnation. I instantly got chills down my spine and I knew without a doubt that my tattoo was Jorge's trigger and his voice mine. My heart melted with love, with the knowledge that we had experienced how God's divine plan works, that our meeting was part of our life's journey. No one has been enamored with my tattoo like Jorge has, and Jorge's voice to me is like listening the most divine music.

I asked Jorge what he felt when he saw my tattoo. He had an "Oh, my God" moment. He dropped his defenses. He read it, read the symbolism behind the ankh, the rose and the snake. He saw that I was clueless about its meaning, the layers and the depth of the three symbols together. He knew, felt deep inside that it was very meaningful and significant. He felt he was given the three symbols that he was obsessed with at the time. He was curious to see what I was like, what my energy was like after seeing that I had three very powerful energetic and ancient symbols tattooed on my leg. He wondered what guided me to get the tattoo without consciously knowing the meaning behind the symbols. He felt that there was genuineness to me. He wondered how it was all connected. He said that he had to know me.

As the week progressed we decided to re-arrange our lives and stay for another week of workshops. It was something that I had never done before, decide something last minute, alter travel plans, and bail on work at the last minute. The chance to spend more time together was something that could not be missed. As the first week ended and the second week began, our deep friendship became romantic and I am so glad that I took the chance and time to be with Jorge. It was no coincidence that we met. I was originally supposed to go to a different workshop in California and he had planned to attend the meditation workshop earlier in the year. Both of our plans changed unexpectedly. I know that this meeting was carefully orchestrated long ago so that we could assist each others' souls in their evolutions. I feel incredibly blessed to have him in my life. It does not mean that things have been easy or painless, but I know that I am working with a true soul mate, and have been given a golden opportunity. I have taken that opportunity without looking back, and it infused my life with endless love, laughter and joy.

Conclusion from Sarina:

In the months since Amy sent me her story, she has moved to Puerto Rico, got married, and is happily living with her beloved Jorge to this day. It is strange, but true.

Selection 3
May To December Romance

By Dorothy Gale

Continued from 1st edition

Economic crisis within a committed relationship

She:

Born 1943, divorced, one adult son

He:

Born 1965, single, no children

Economy on the edge

We have heard our parents and grandparents talk about the Great Depression. We've read about it in our history books. We've seen documentaries on television describing the devastation that took place during this historical period. Did we ever think for a moment that we would actually experience that very same thing in our lifetimes? Not a chance. We neglected to heed the words of the great philosopher, George Santayana, when he clearly warned, "Those who cannot remember the past are condemned to repeat it."

Unexpected Unemployment

Both he and she were employed for ten years by the same employer; working side by side and enjoying a fine salary. Their life-style surely wasn't extravagant, but they were able to live fairly well without worry. Dining out, theatre, concerts, and social events were part of their frequent regimen. Then, without warning, they were both terminated on the same day. No severance, just good-bye and good luck. The economy had taken its toll and the company they spent all of those years with simply folded. Never anticipating this and most certainly not planning for it, they were both frozen in a state of shock. "Other people" had fallen on hard times – this couldn't be happening to them – not both at the same time!

Plan? What Plan?

They spent the better part of the following week occasionally and silently glancing at one another – hoping the other had a "plan" in place, just in case this current scenario might present itself some time in the future. What immediately presented itself were a looming mortgage, credit card bills, utility bills, auto and insurance payments, and everyday needs. It became immediately clear that groceries would now become more of a luxury vs. necessity. Clipping coupons from the Sunday newspaper and fliers in the mail would become part of the daily routine. Surfing the Internet each morning upon waking and searching job boards was the first order of business. Networking became a tedious chore. They found that people in their network who were gainfully employed actually had fewer resources and suggestions than those who were in the same position as they were. The future looked bleak with each newscast. The economy was in grave trouble and the unemployment rate was increasing rapidly by the day. Statistics tell us that financial problems within a relationship are the leading cause of divorce and/or break-ups. The stress involved is staggering and debilitating. One must keep a level head under these circumstances and attempt to maintain calm. Easier said than done.

Fast Forward One Year Later

Commitment in a relationship is tested continually. Affection doesn't come easily and as frequently. Laughter and enjoyment together is sporadic. Sex? Remembering the last time is a painful effort. Still unemployed, but both have found odd jobs here and there to barely stay afloat. The love of friends has become clearly obvious, and the help on any level has been received with profound gratitude. The love for one another has not changed and the commitment to each other has been the sail that keeps the lifeboat on course over the rocky waves of occasional depression and stress. Whatever happens in the not-too-distant future is the destiny of two people sharing adversity and difficult times. That, my friends, is commitment.

Chapter 9

Play The Game

So many of you tell me you're sick and tired of being let down, betrayed, and hurt by love. You put your best effort forward and get dumped anyway. You tell the truth, and get lied to. You open your heart, and some idiot steps all over it. Right?

So, what's next? You just shut down? Oh, maybe some casual sex here and there. Perhaps, even, a short lived interest or two, but basically, you're closed for business?

Come on! That's part of the game! We're not children, we know this! If we don't take risks, we miss the good stuff. Even if you are educated in psychology or travel the world looking for an easy path to love, there are risks. With risk comes potential failure. Or, is it really failure when it comes to love?

We've all been there. The pain of rejection is staggering, isn't it? It stings like hell to be lied to by a lover. Dating one of those Personality Types from The Tao of Intimacy book is almost a joke, but we get sucked in anyway, because it's exciting!

Look, I see two kinds of lovers; a) the ones who feel victimized by love, and b) the ones who learn from their mistakes and grow. Which kind are you?

I have interviewed countless couples, and take my word for it; pain and disappointment are part of human interaction. But, so is lounging in bed until noon with your sweetie. Laughing together, taking walks, and yummy sex are also part of the dating game. Would you honestly give up those wonderful memories just because it didn't work out? I say "Heck no!"

So, buck up boys and girls. This is the stuff they write poetry and songs about. I have traveled the globe and been courted by some amazing men, all of whom have left wonderful memories which cause me to smile secretly to myself sometimes. Of course, there was pain. But long after the sting of separation flees, these lovely images remain mine. It is these images of laughter, sharing, passion and conflict that fuel my faith in love to this day; long after my handsome Romeos have gone.

So, there you have it. If you need to take a little time to restore your faith, take it. And when you are ready, put a smile on your beautiful face, hold your head up like an adult; open your heart and play, play, play!

www.ingramcontent.com/pod-product-compliance
Lightning Source LLC
Chambersburg PA
CBHW060853280326
41934CB00007B/1037